This coloring book belongs to:

_ _ _ _ _ _ _ _ _ _ _ _

Copyright 2021 StayMagical
All rights reserved
No part of this book may be reproduced or used in any manner without the proper written permission of the copyright owner.

LETTERS AND ANIMALS

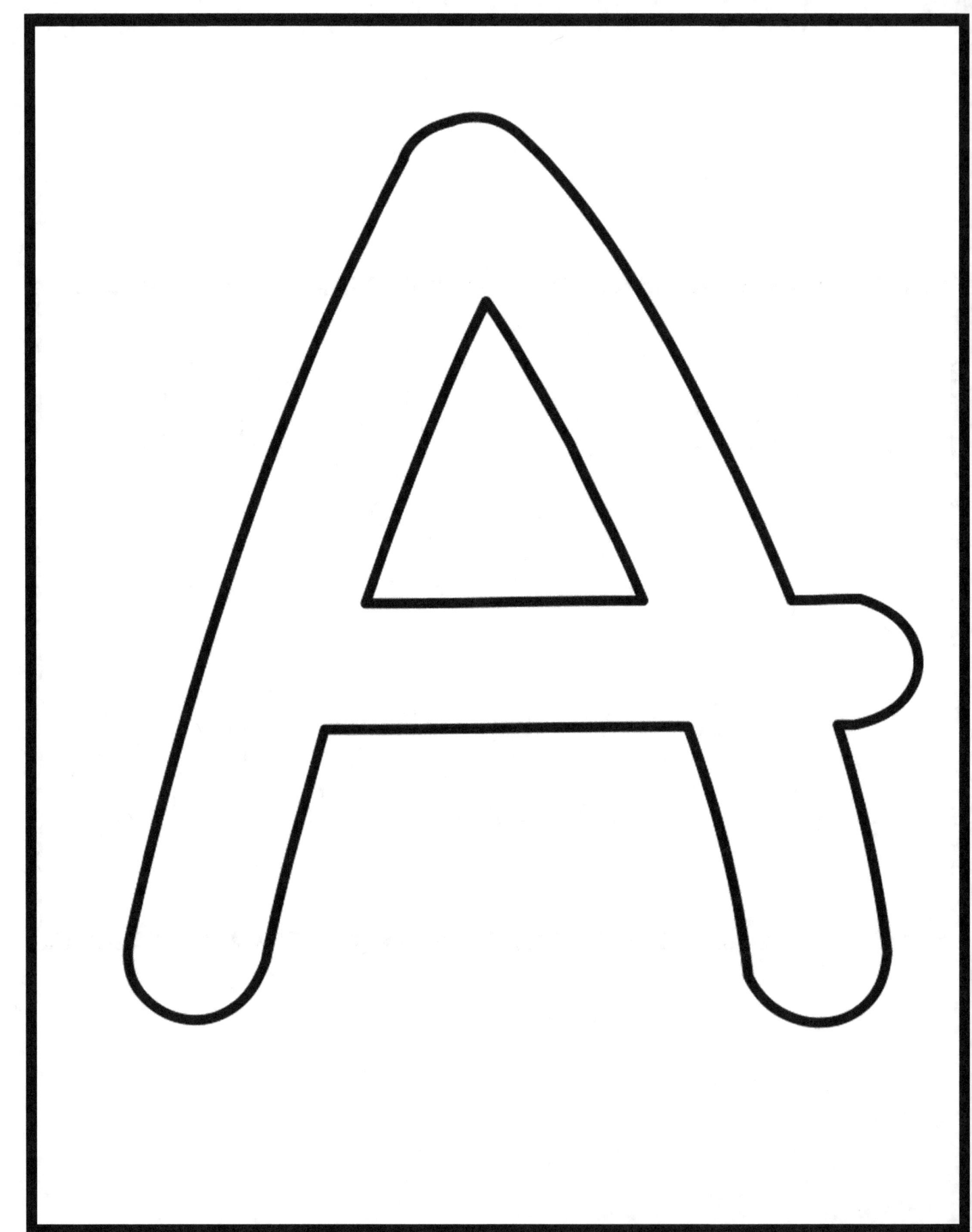

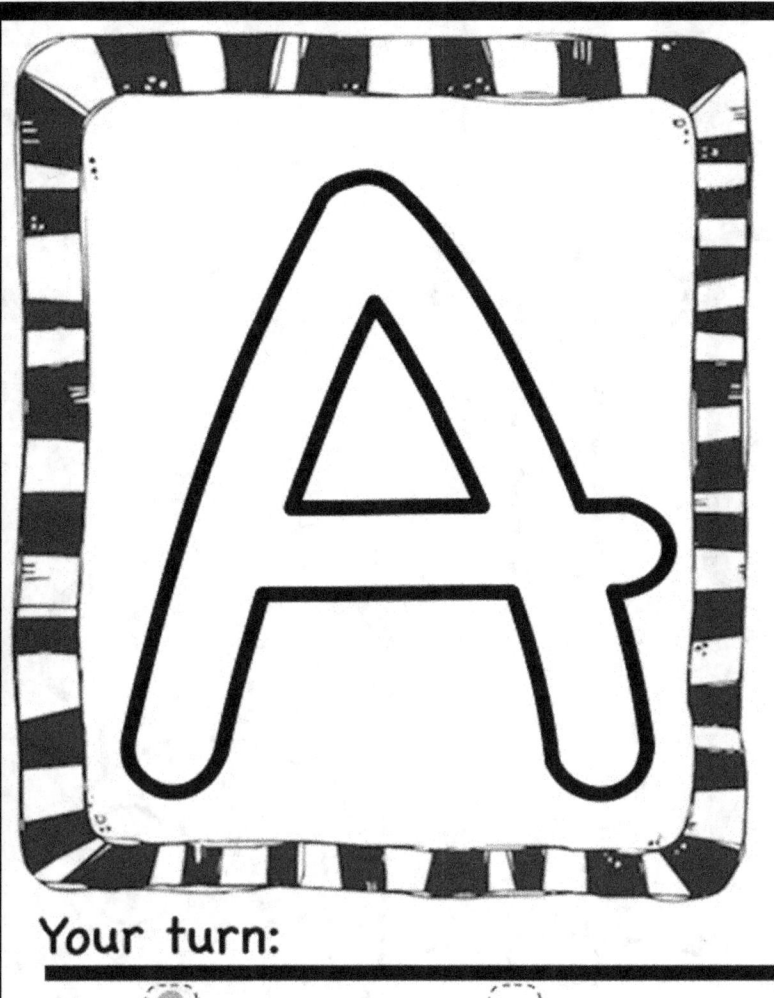

Uppercase

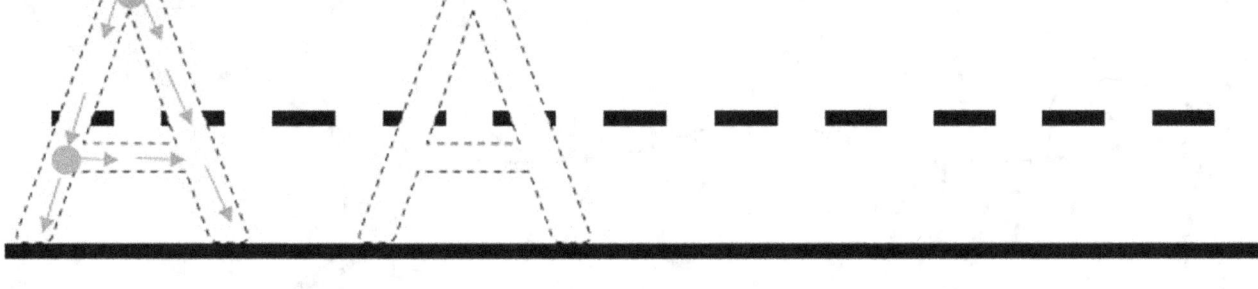

Lowercase

Your turn:

ANT

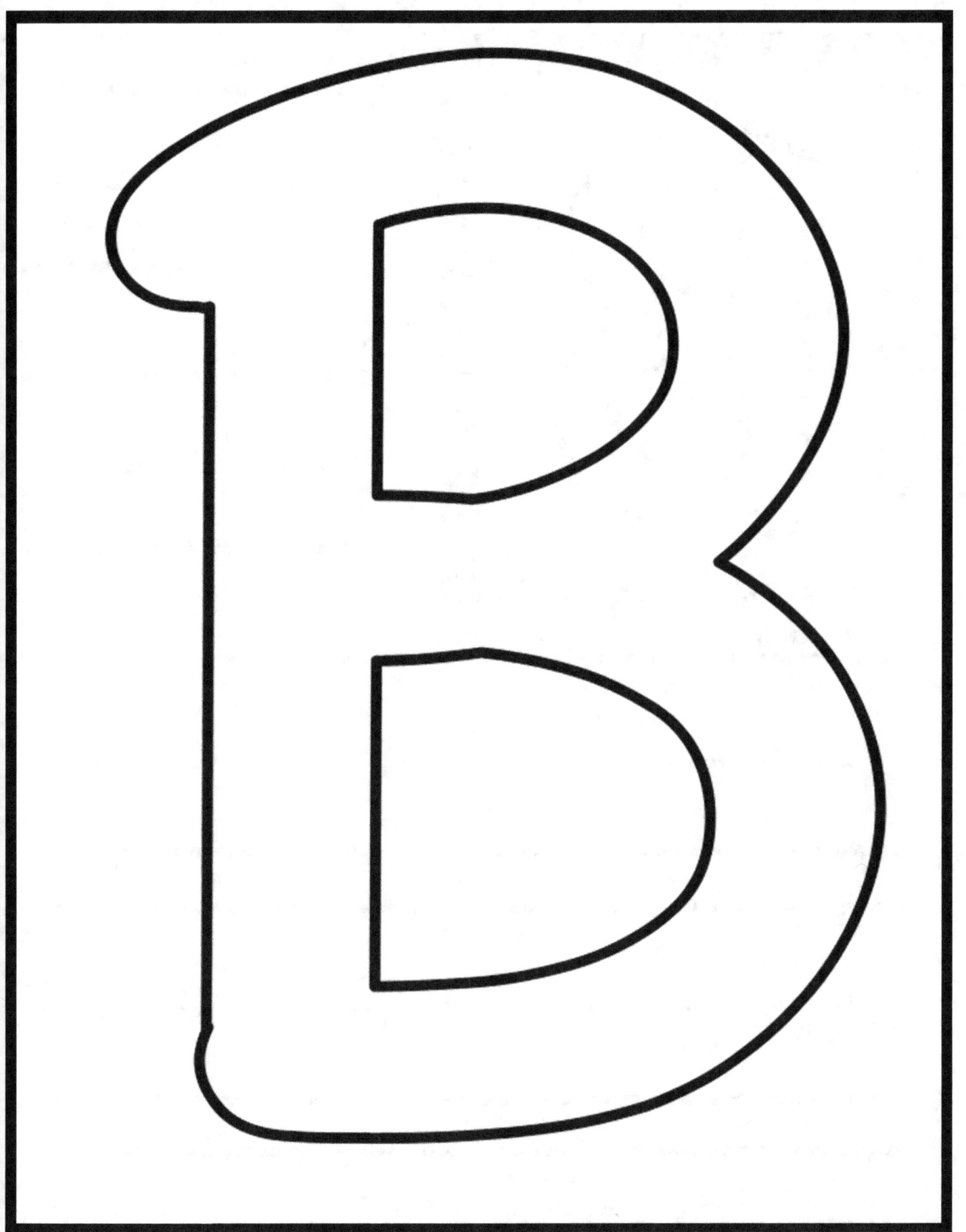

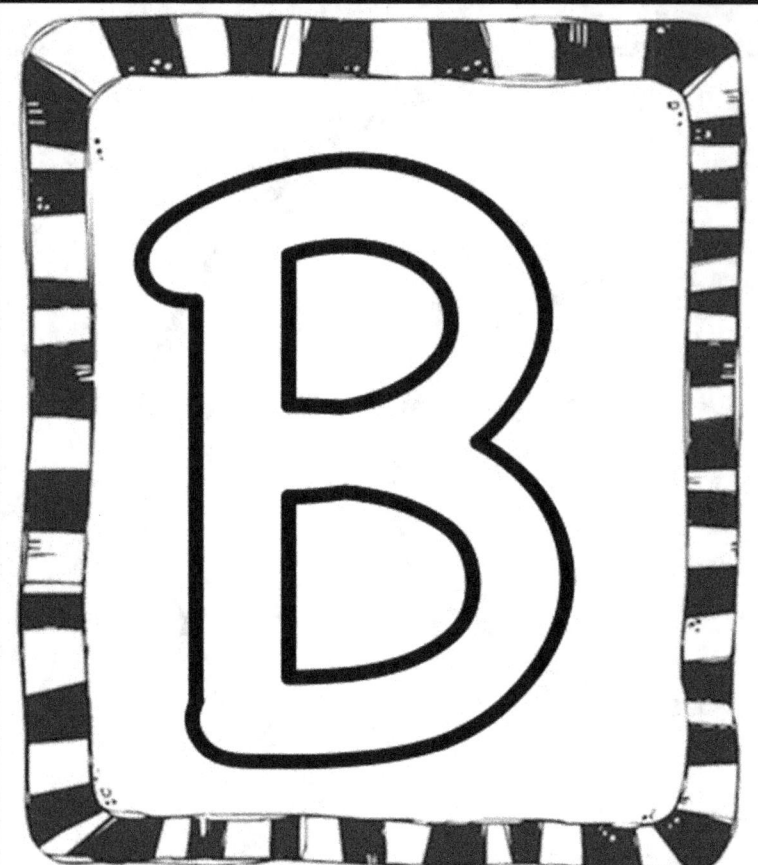

Uppercase

Lowercase

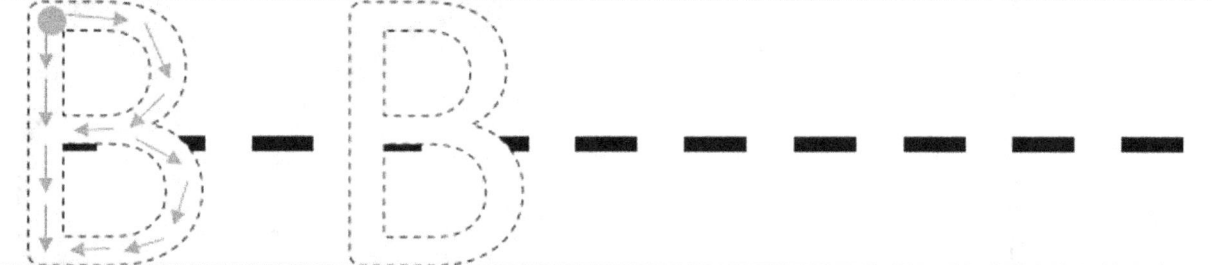

Your turn:

BEAVER

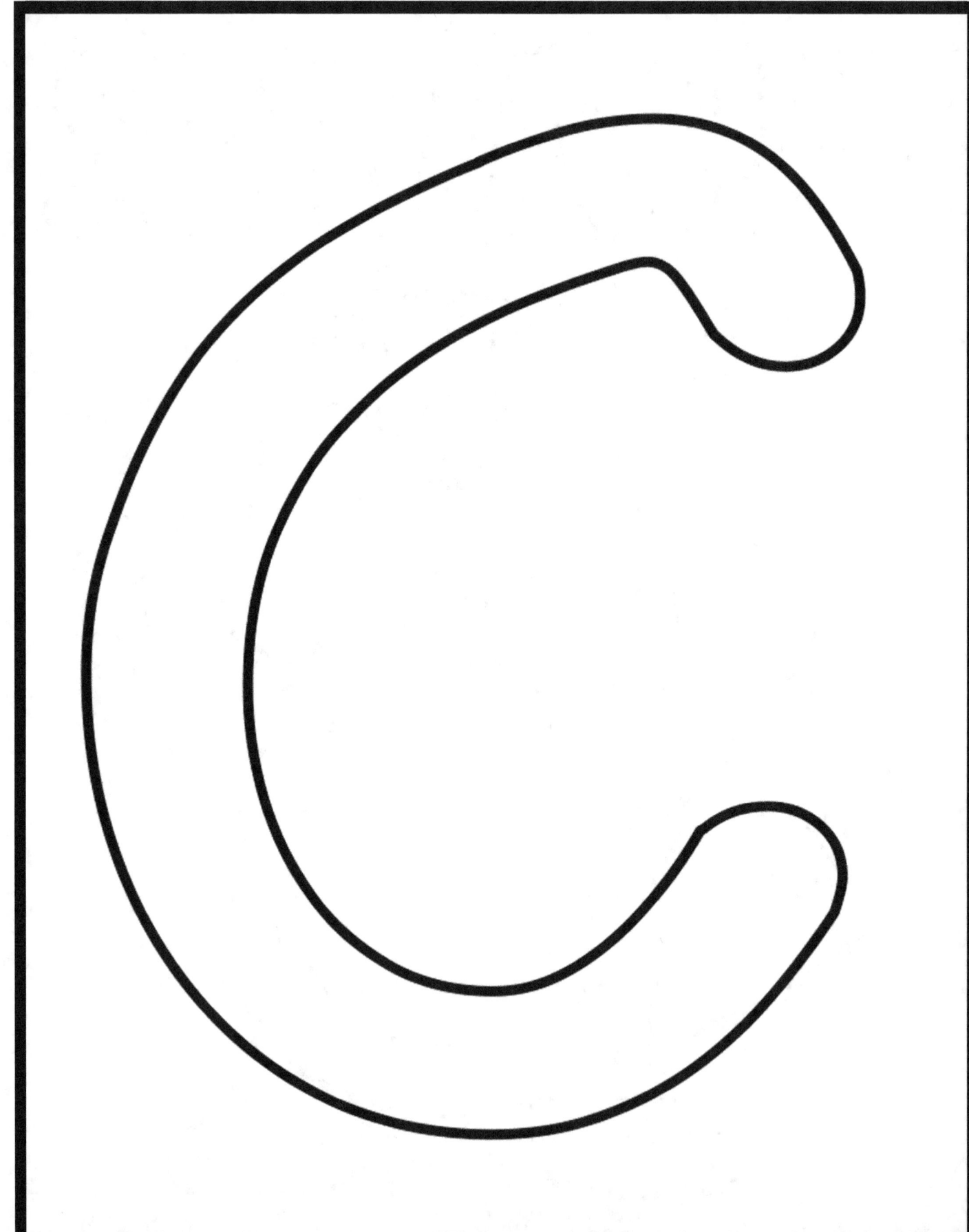

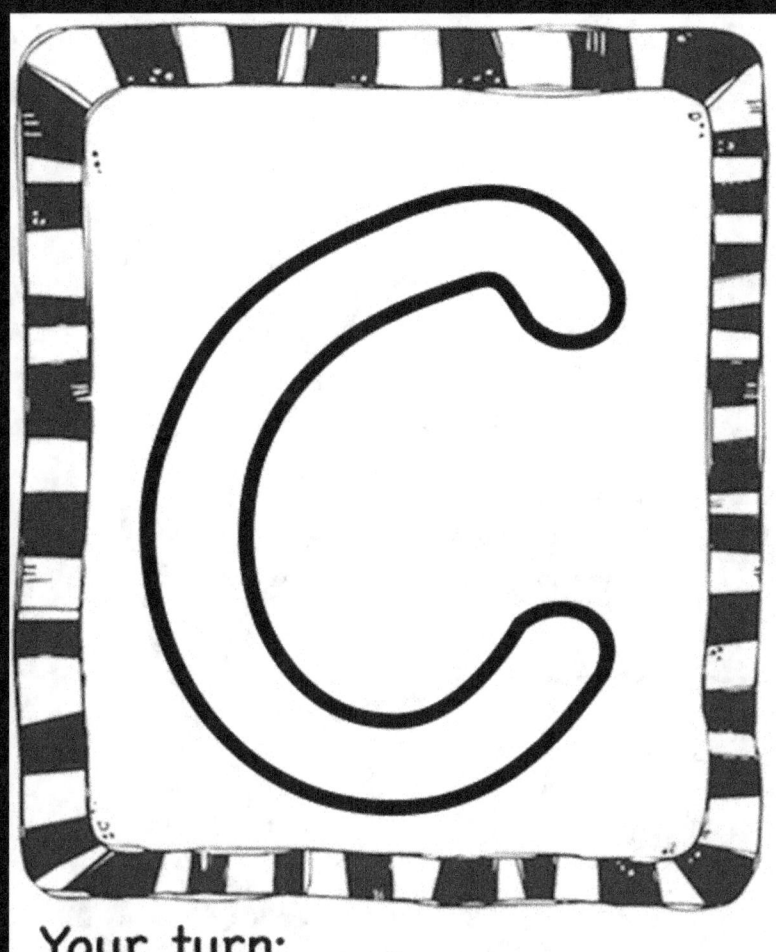

Uppercase

C c c

Lowercase

c c c

Your turn:

c c

c c

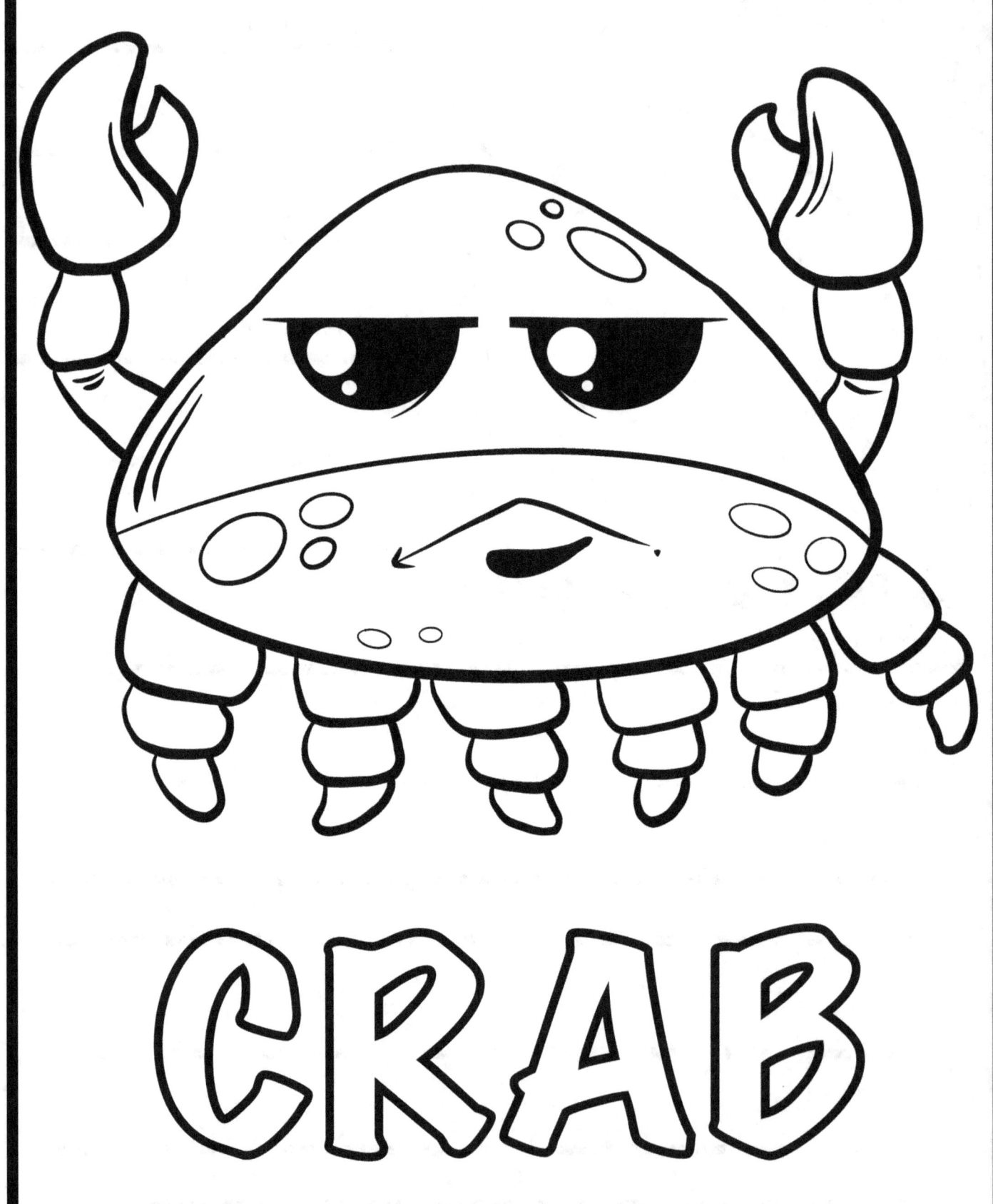

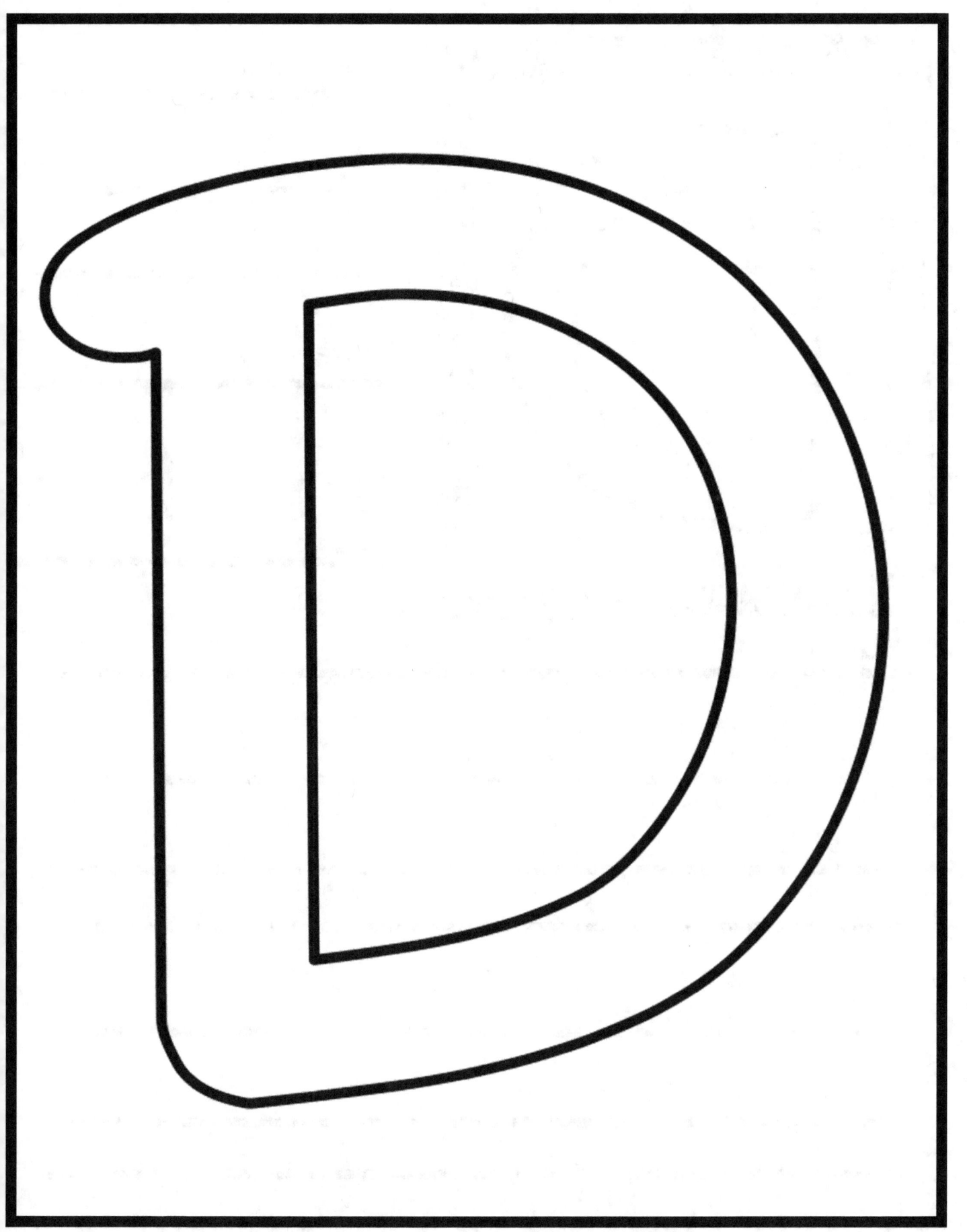

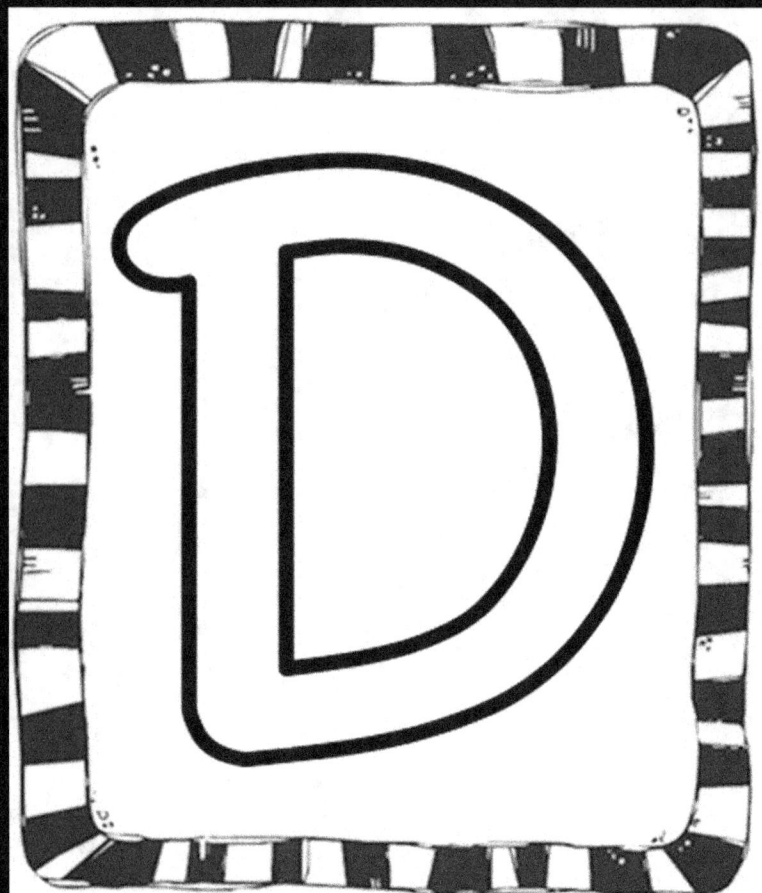

Uppercase

D D D

Lowercase

d d d

Your turn:

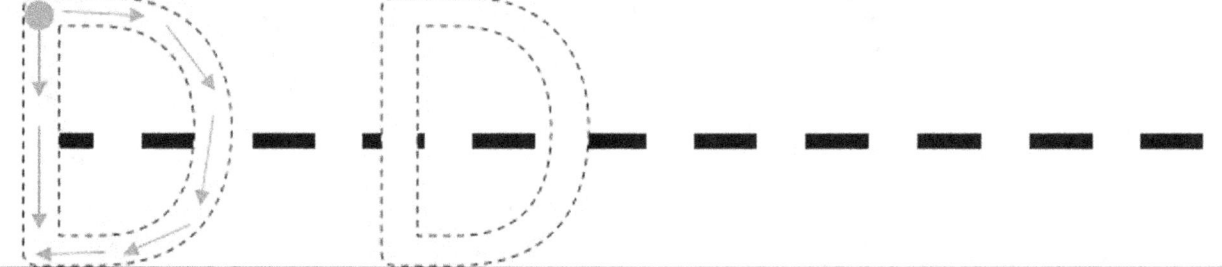

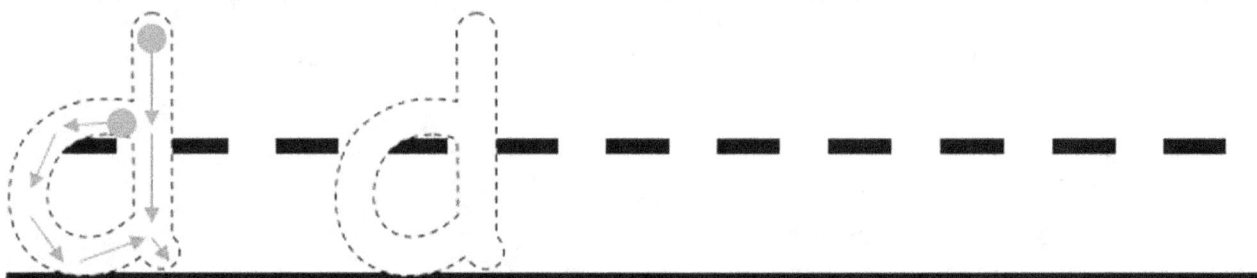

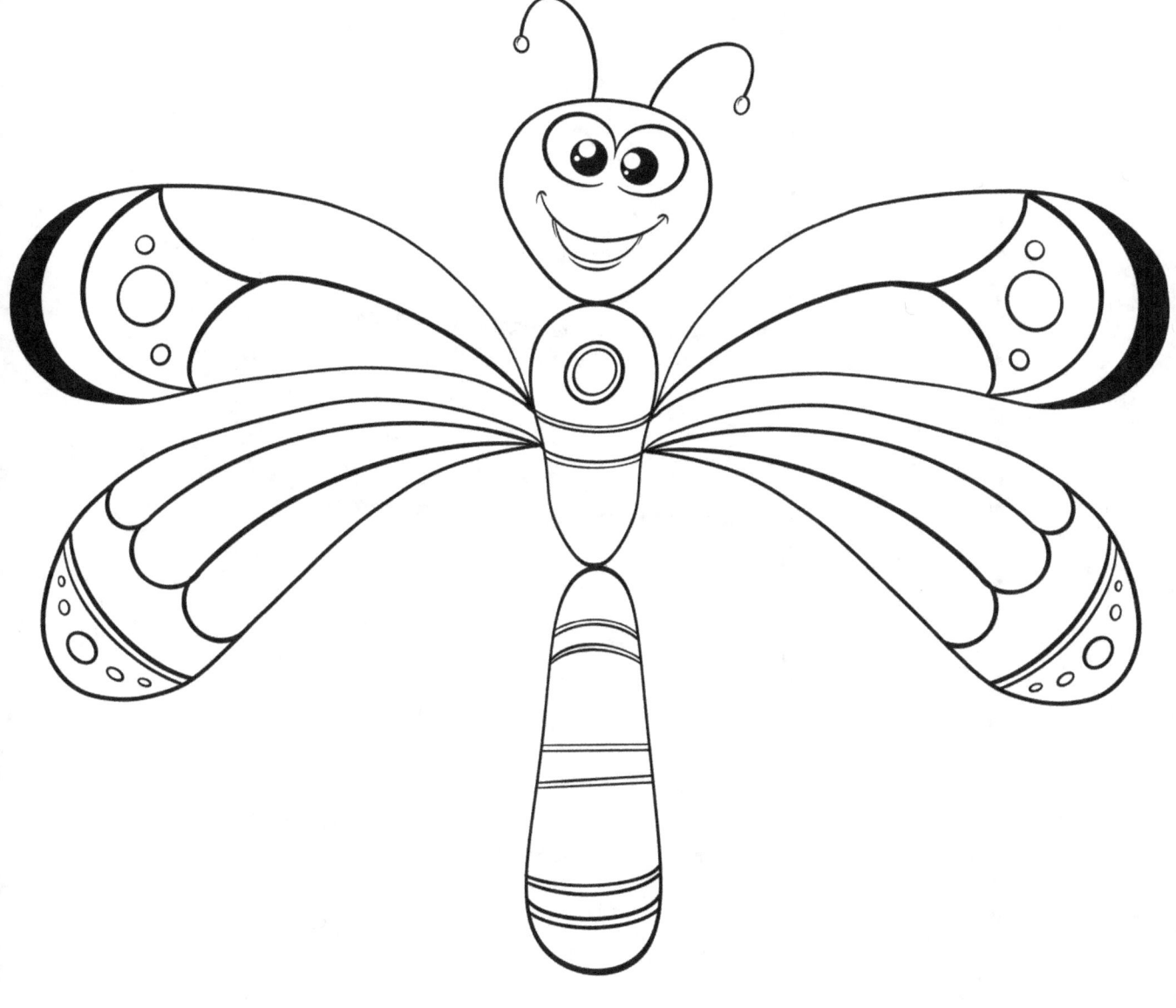

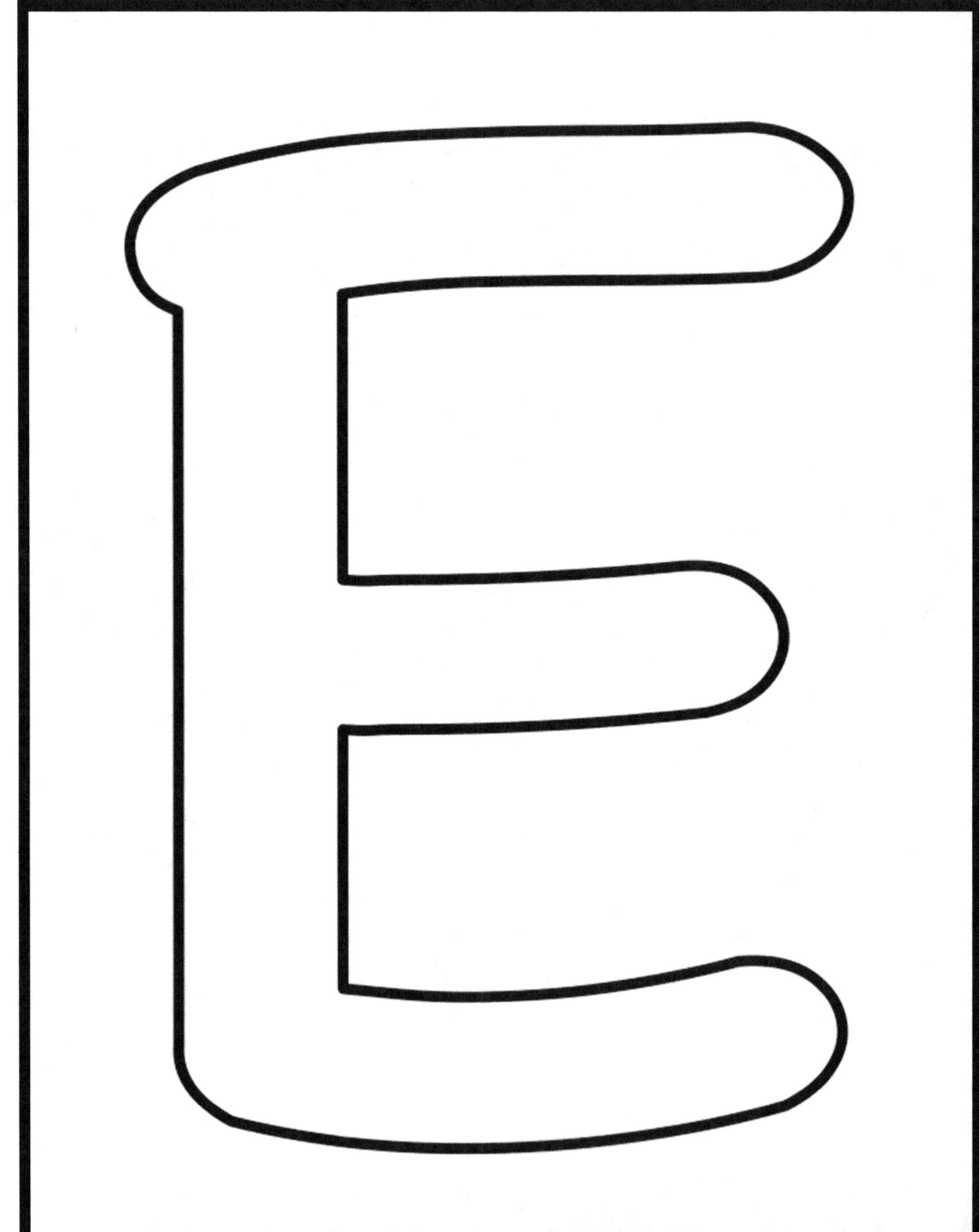

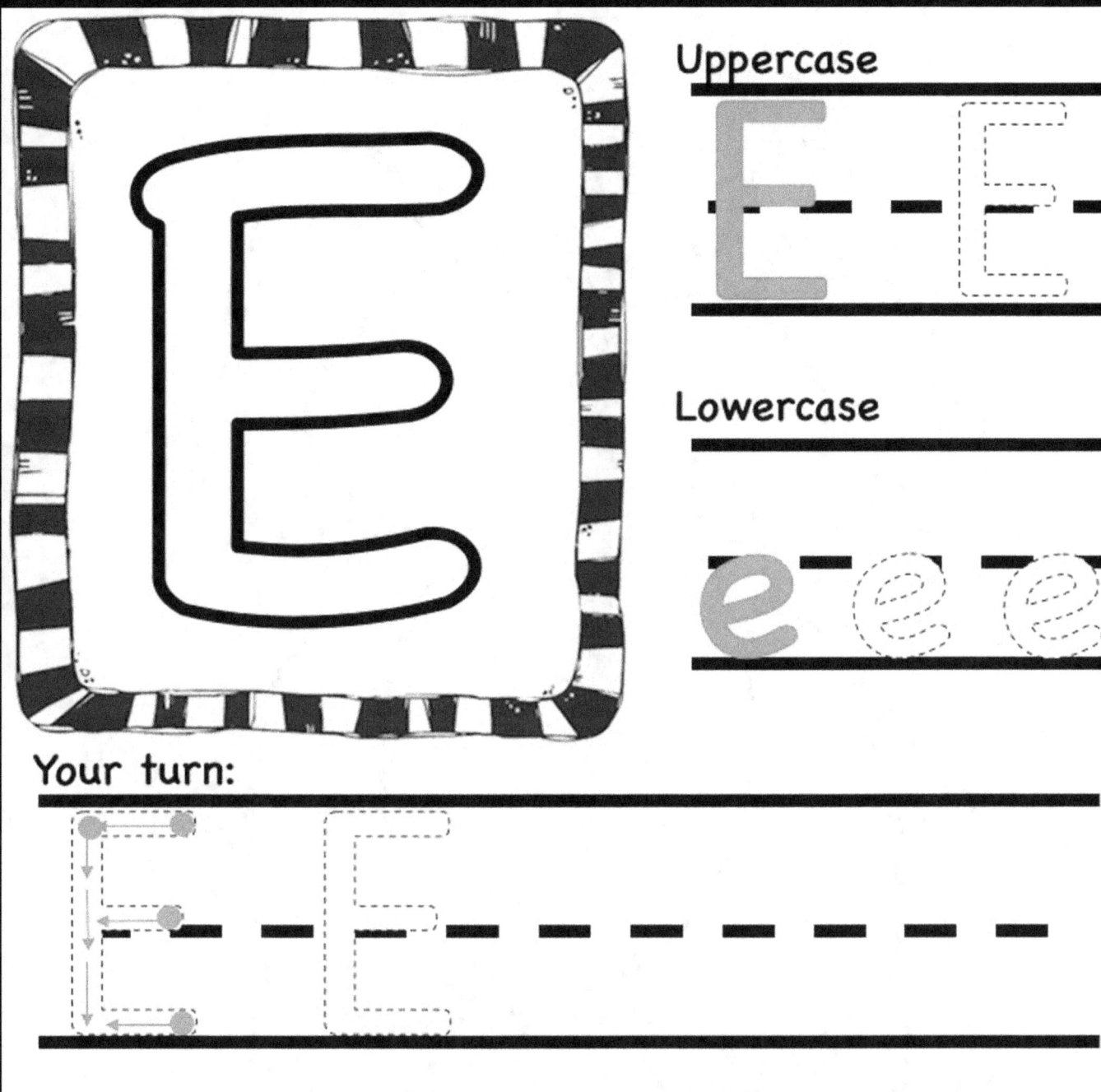

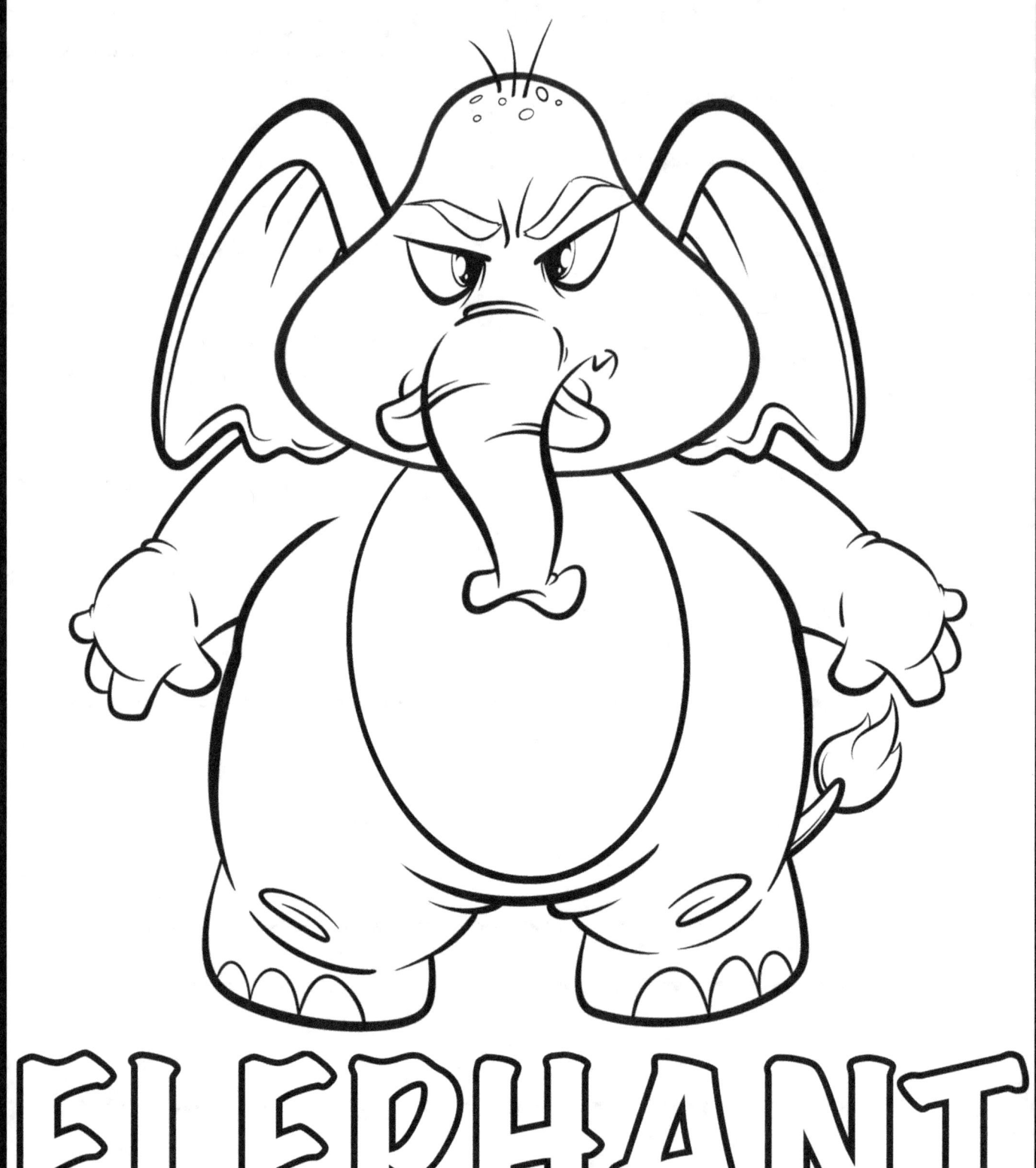

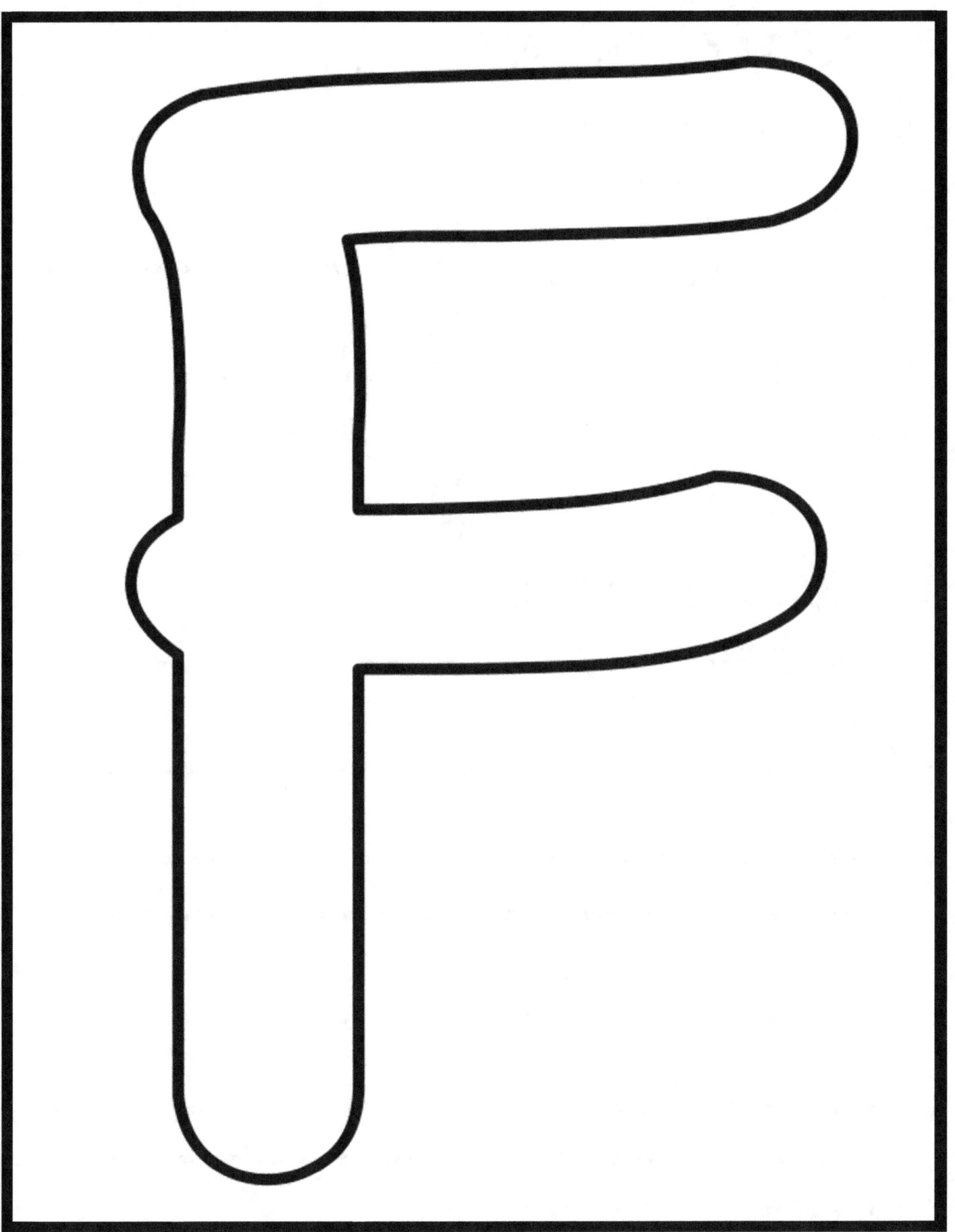

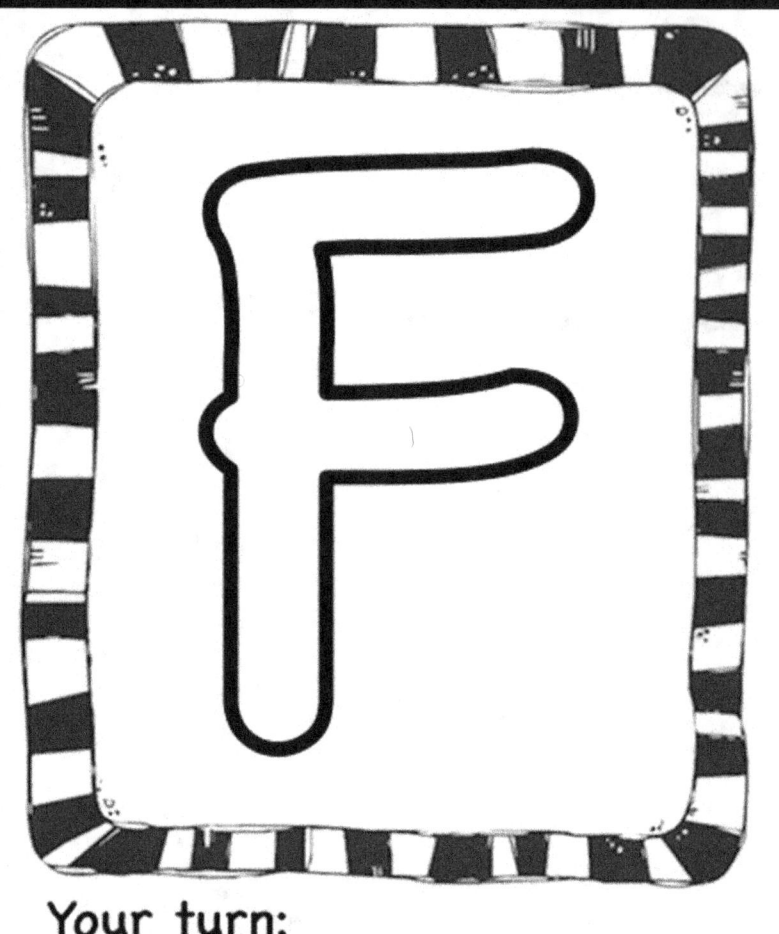

Uppercase

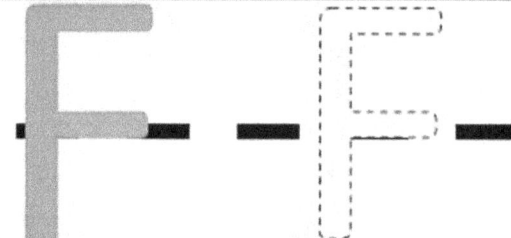

Lowercase

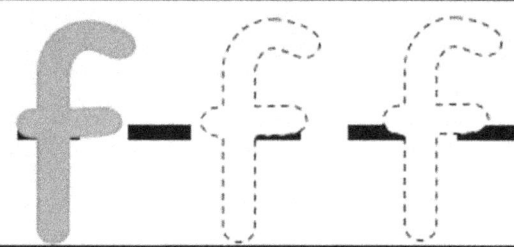

Your turn:

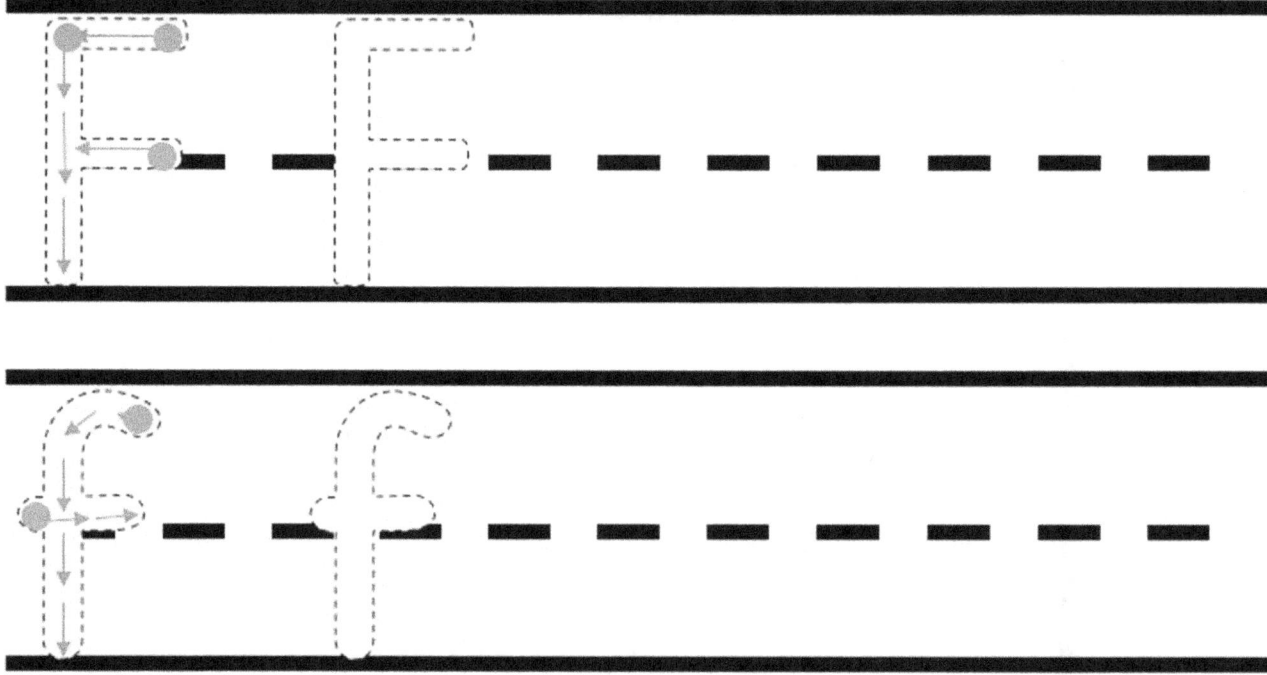

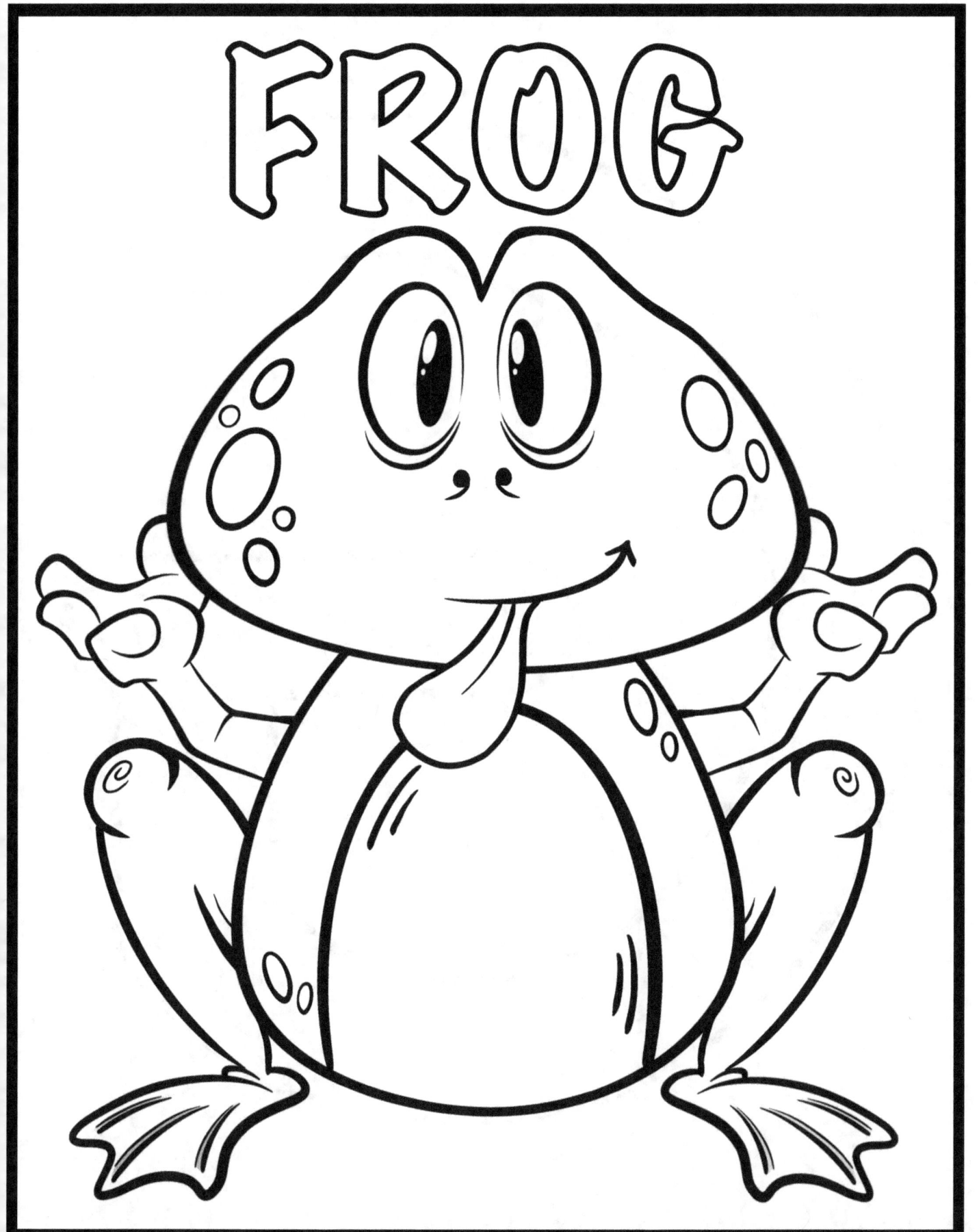

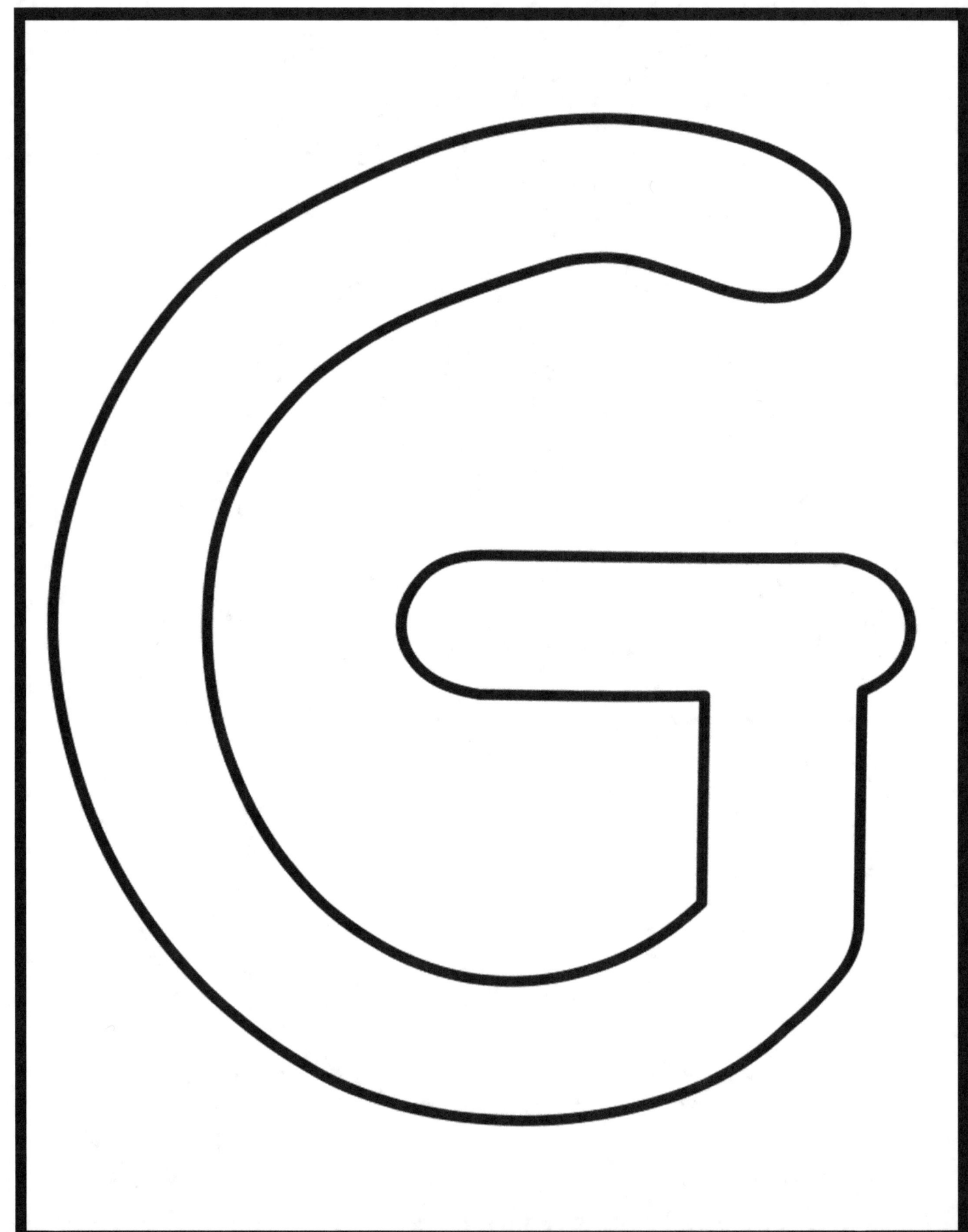

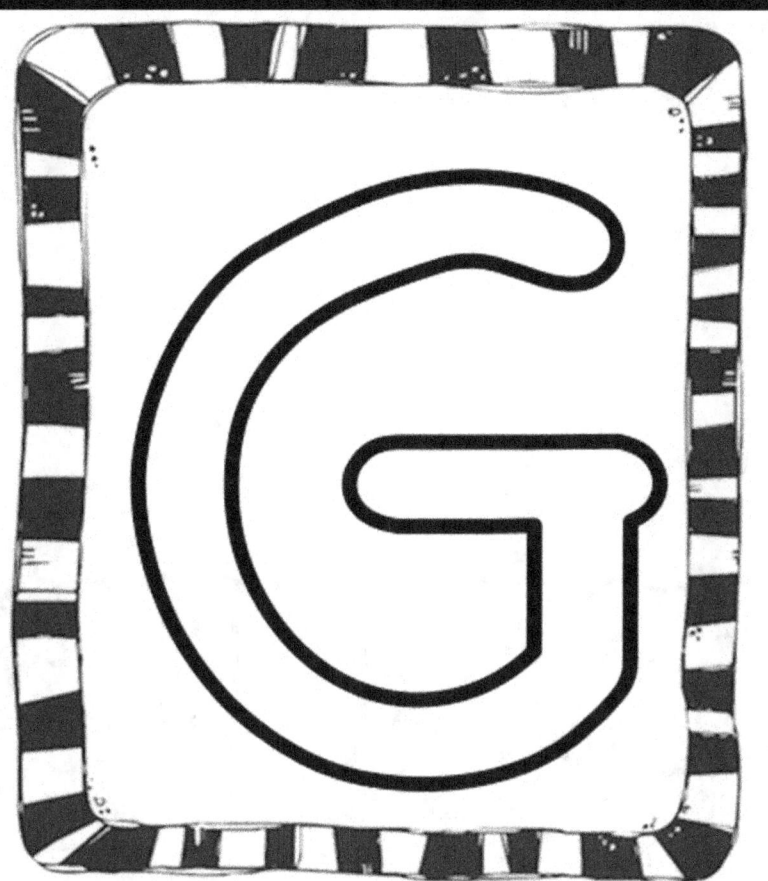

Uppercase

G G G

Lowercase

g g g

Your turn:

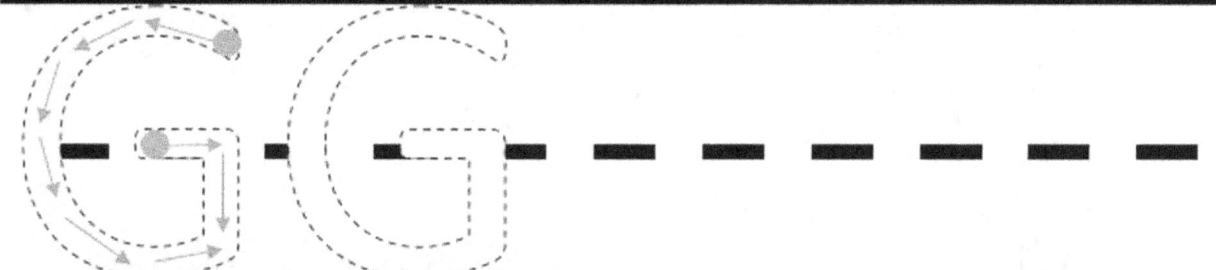

G G G

g g

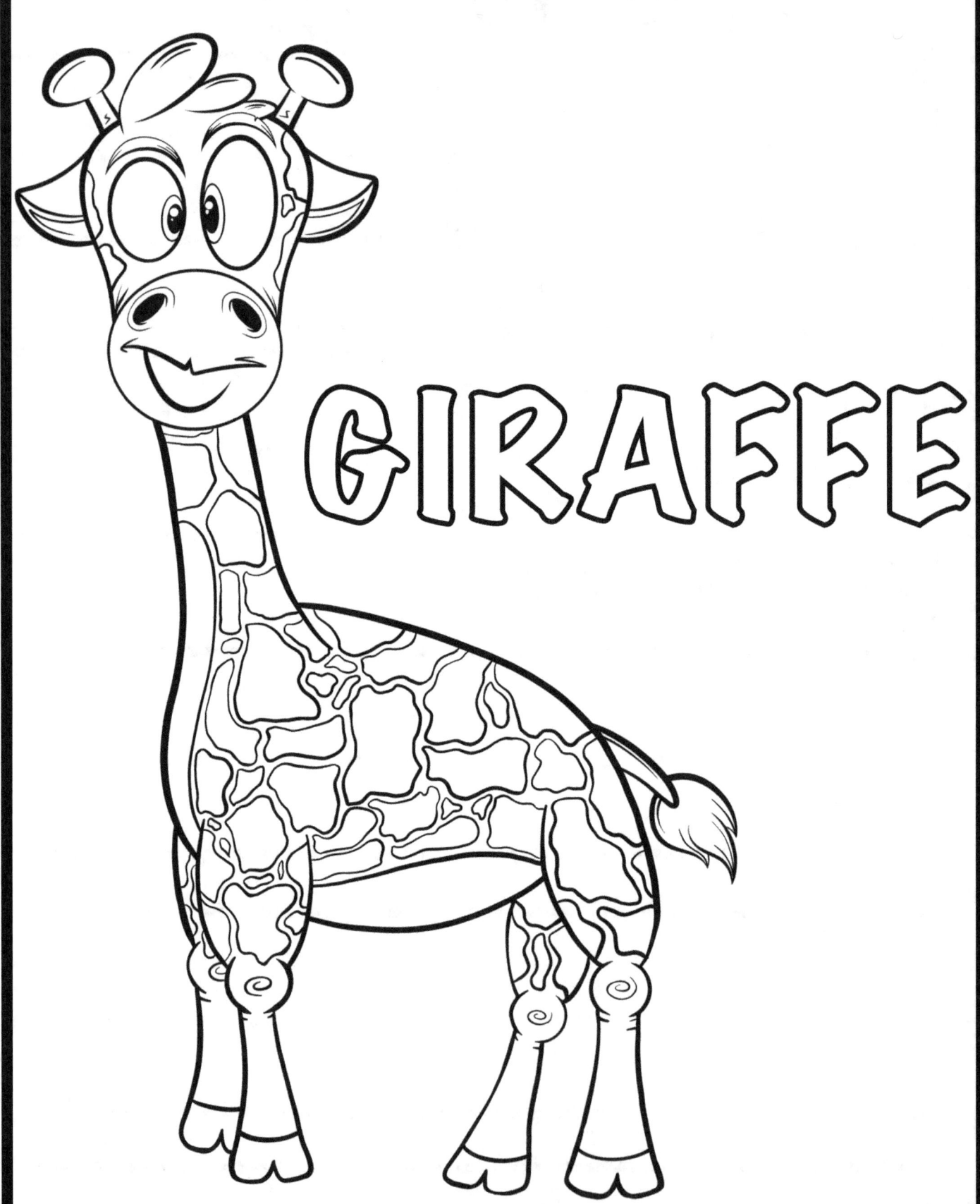

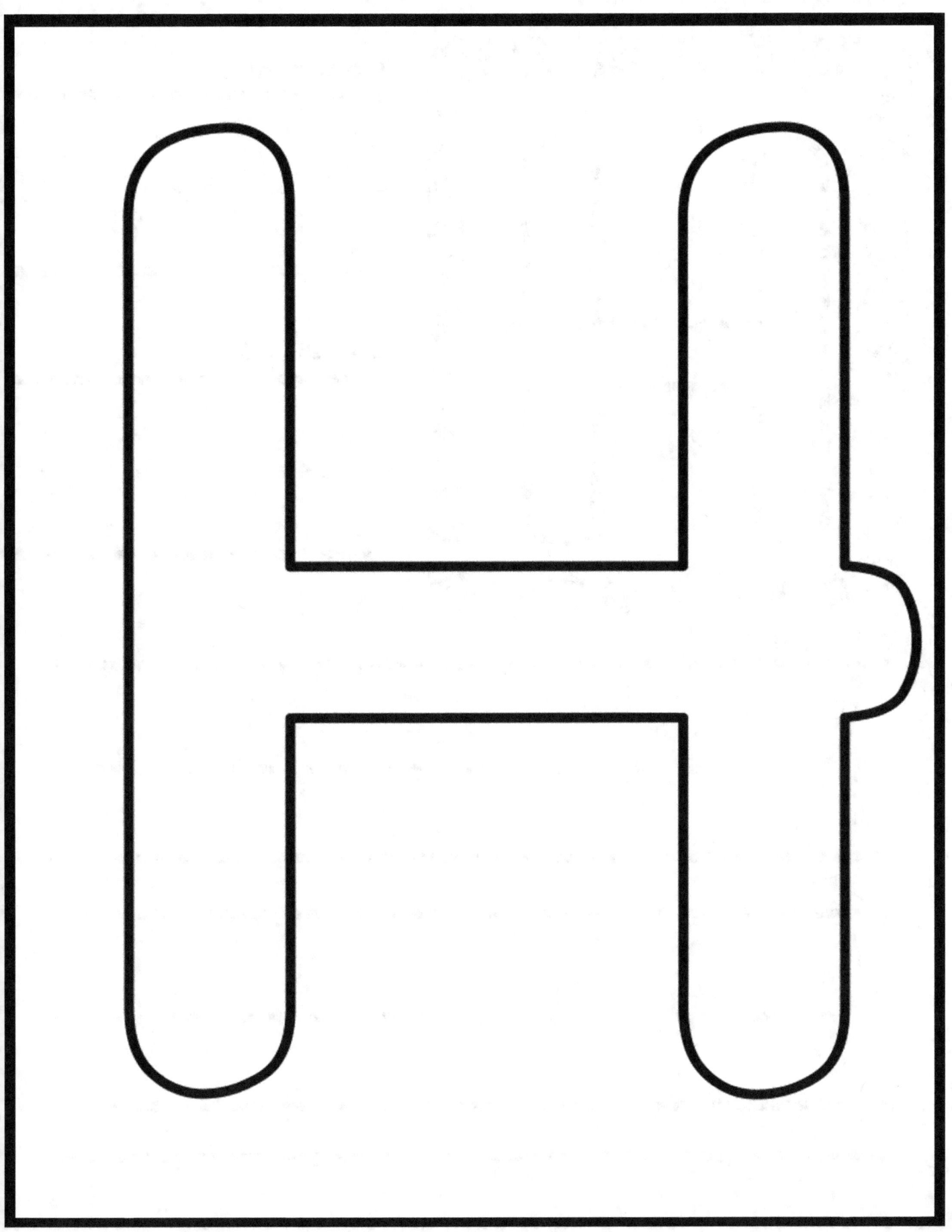

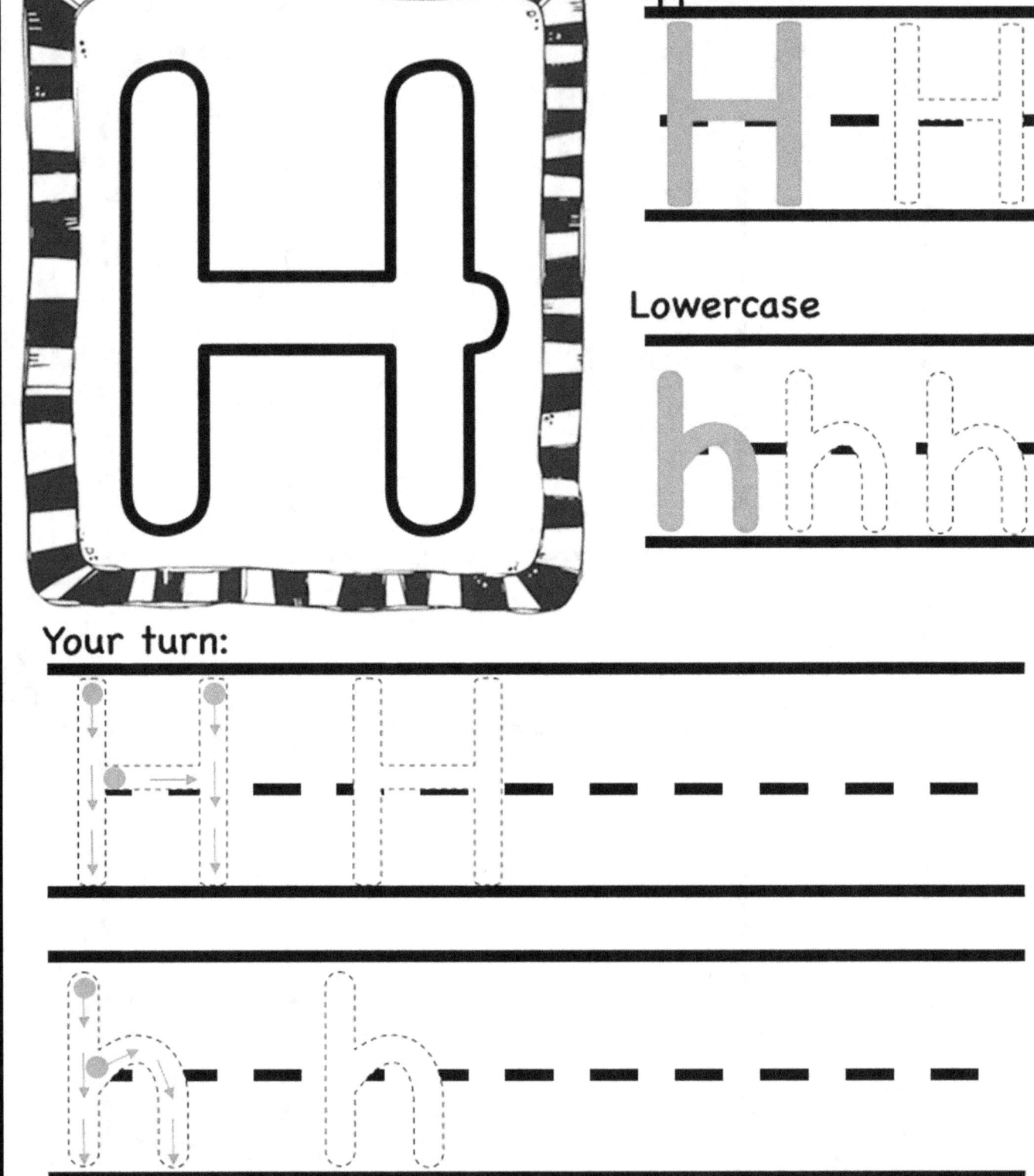

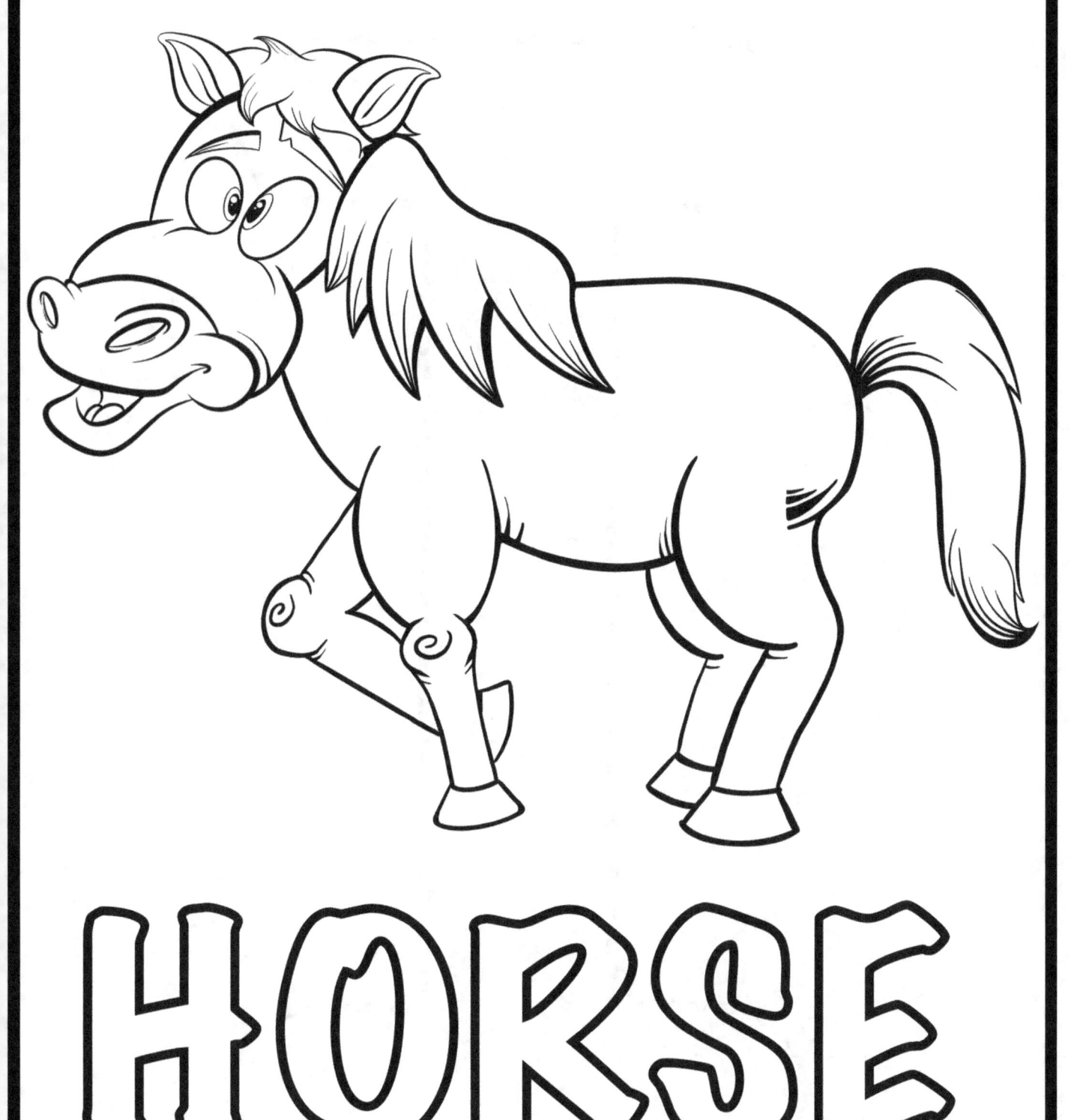

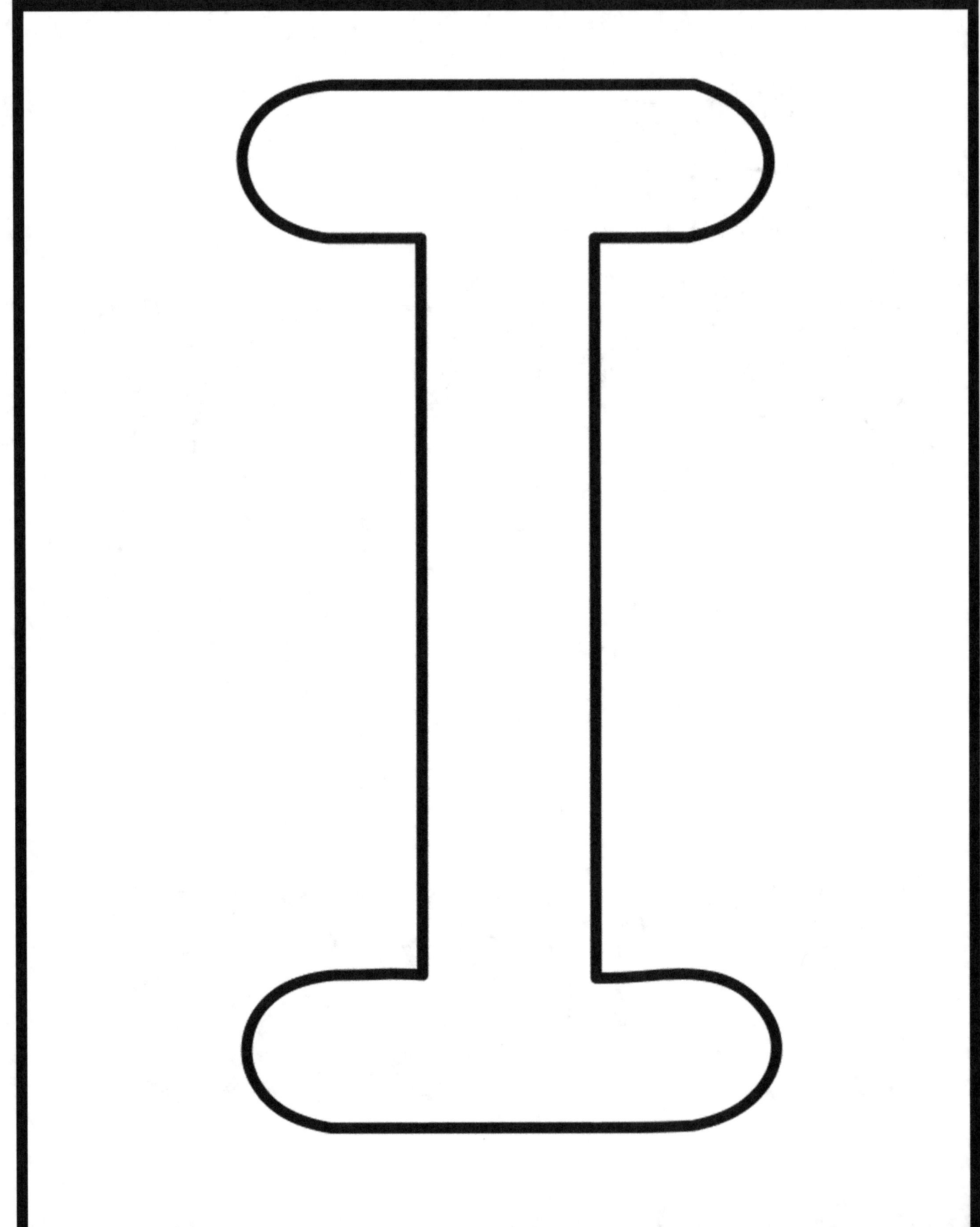

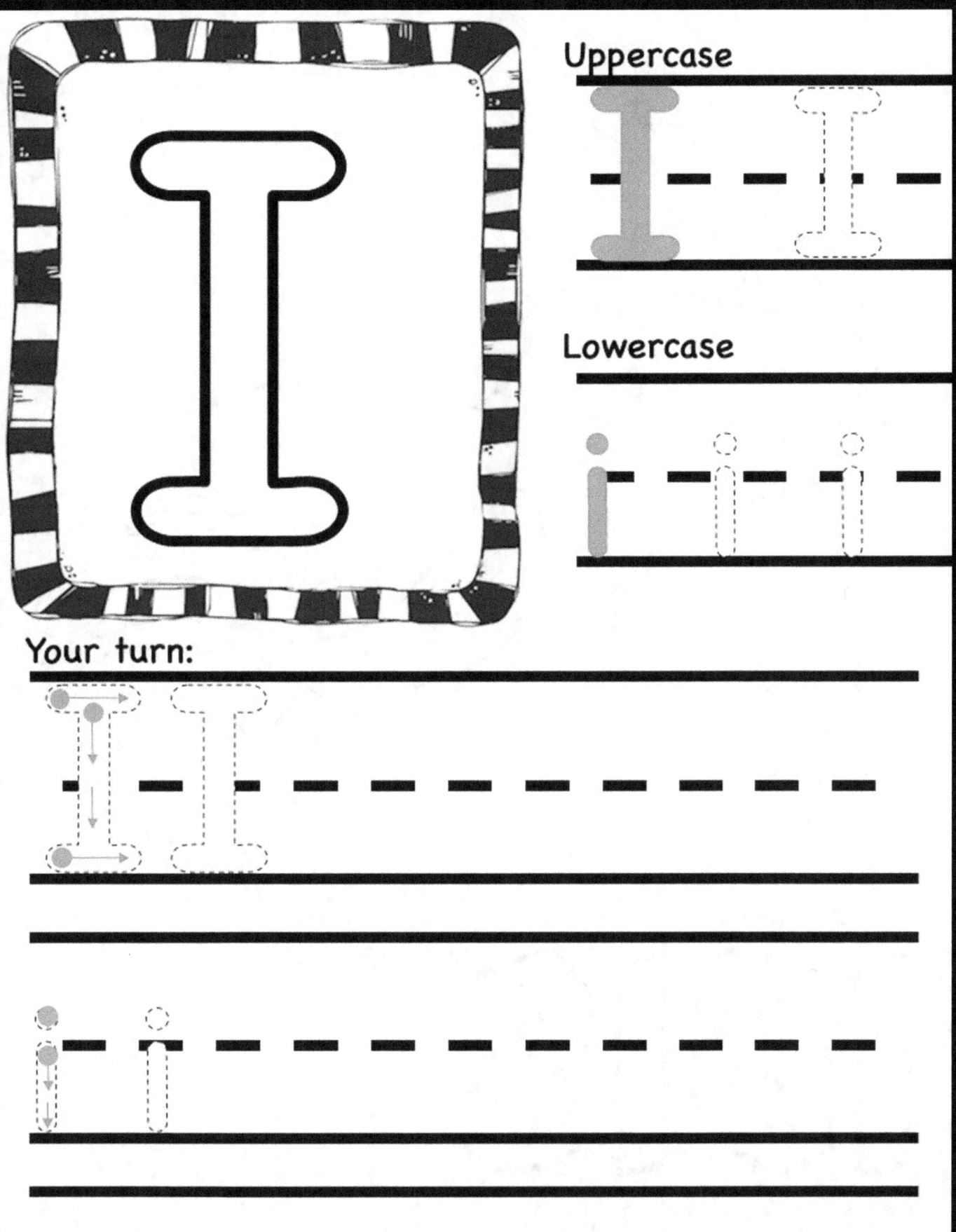

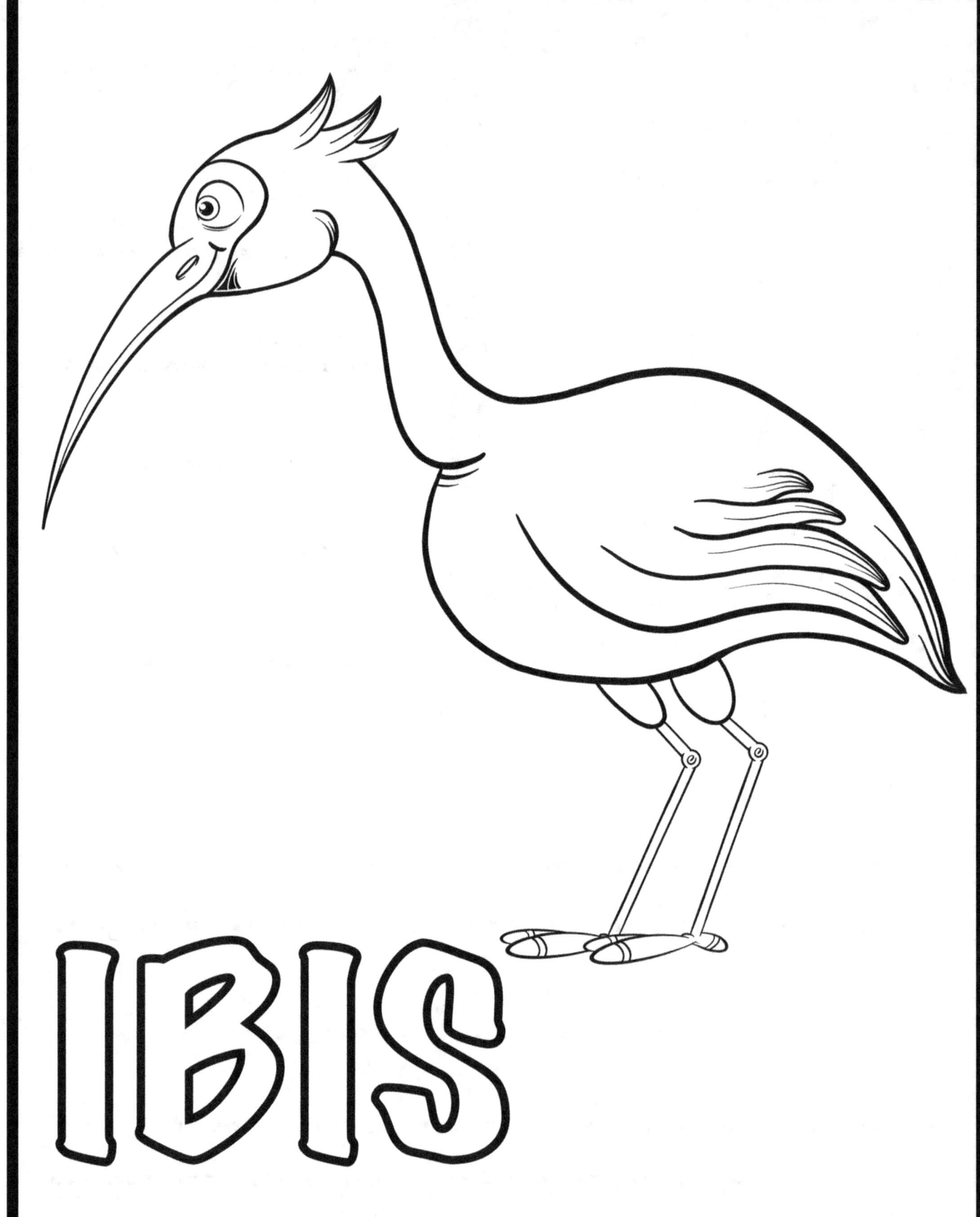

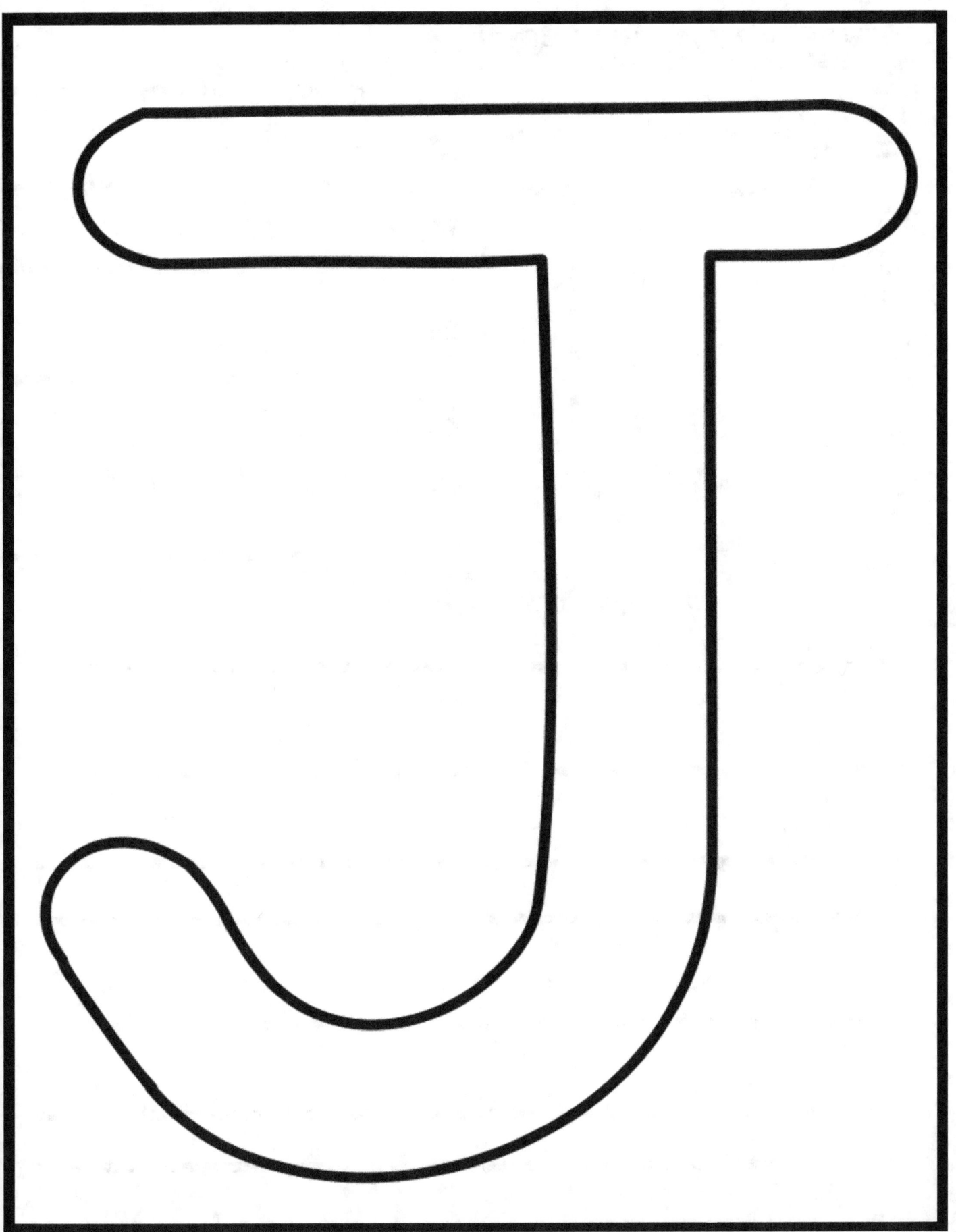

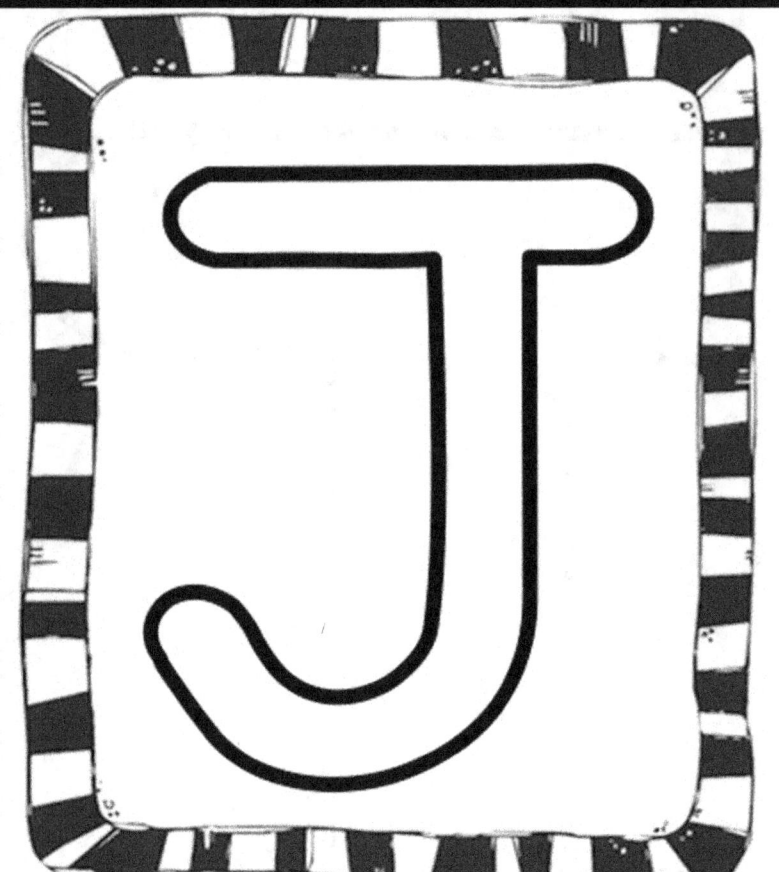

Uppercase

Lowercase

Your turn:

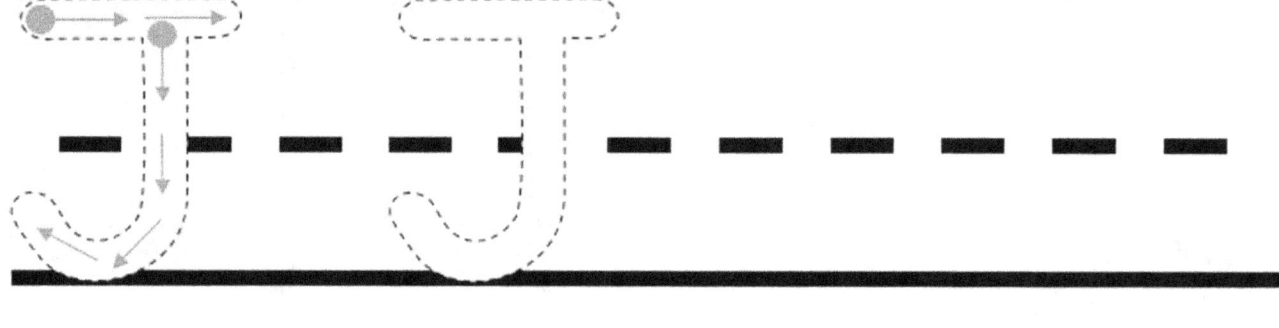

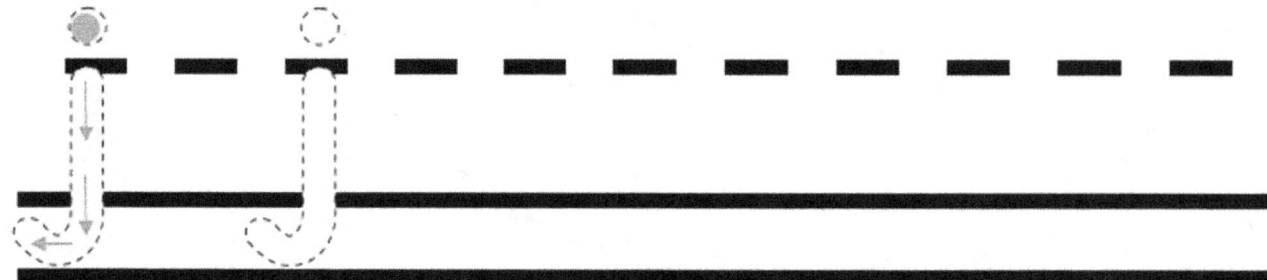

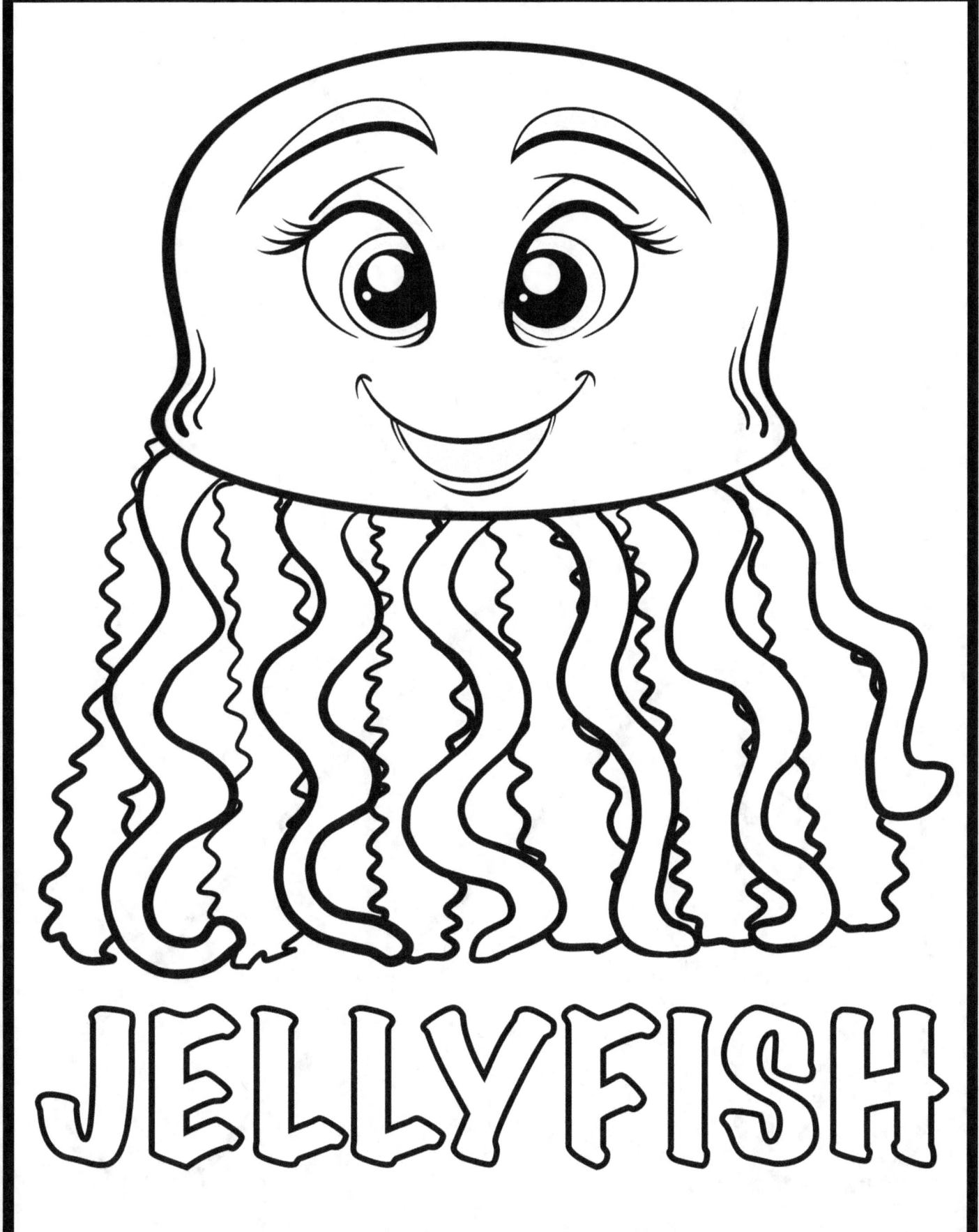

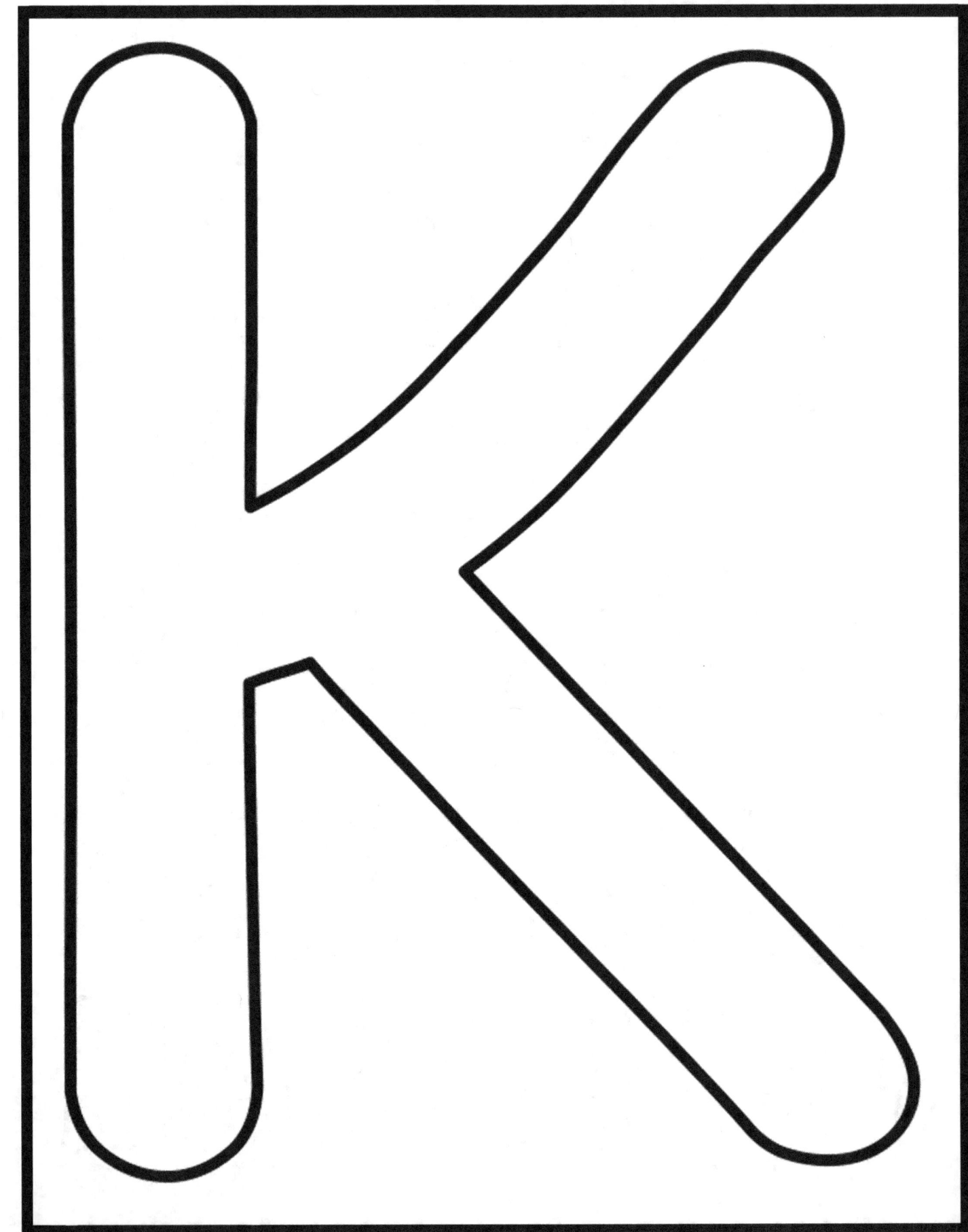

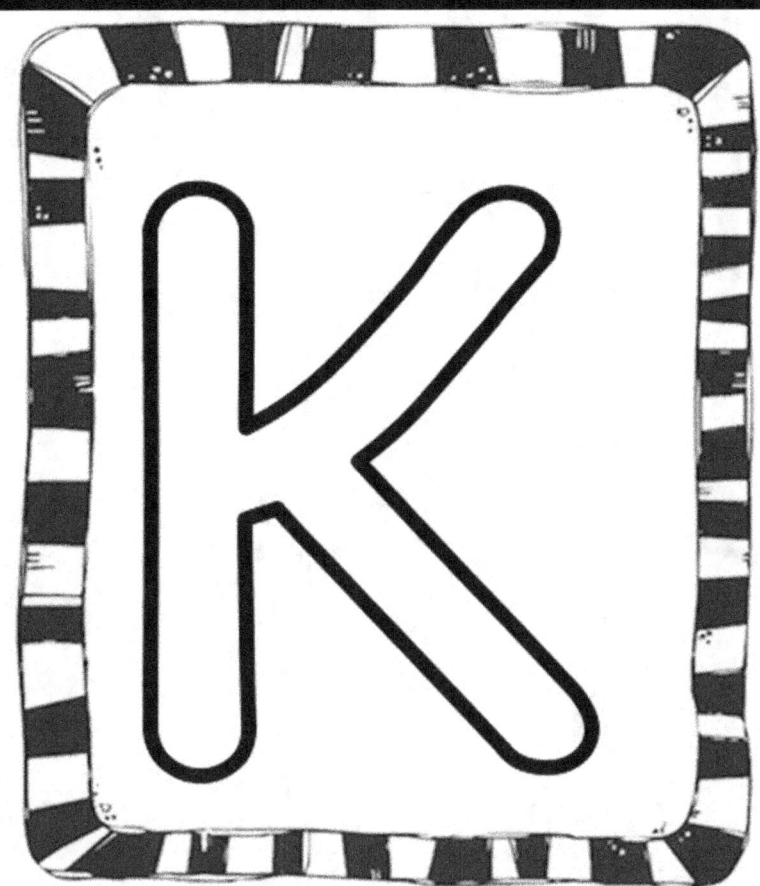

Uppercase

K - K - K

Lowercase

k - k - k

Your turn:

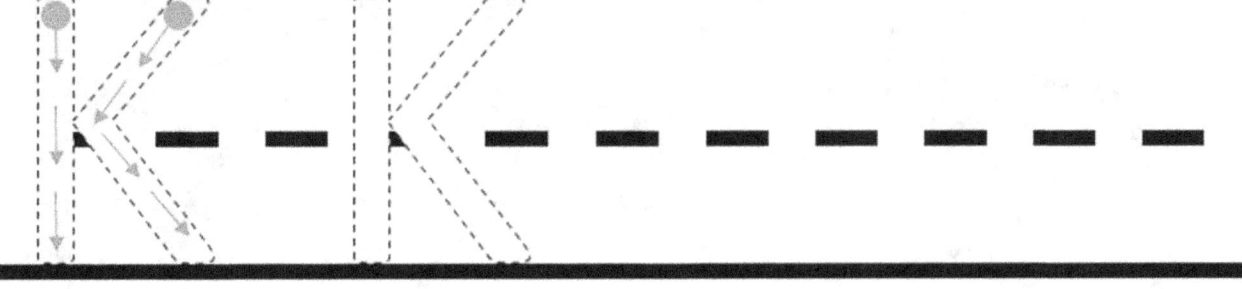

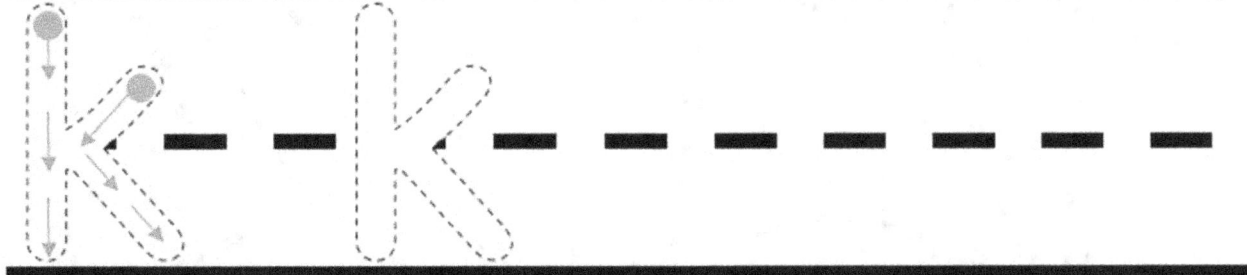

KITTEN

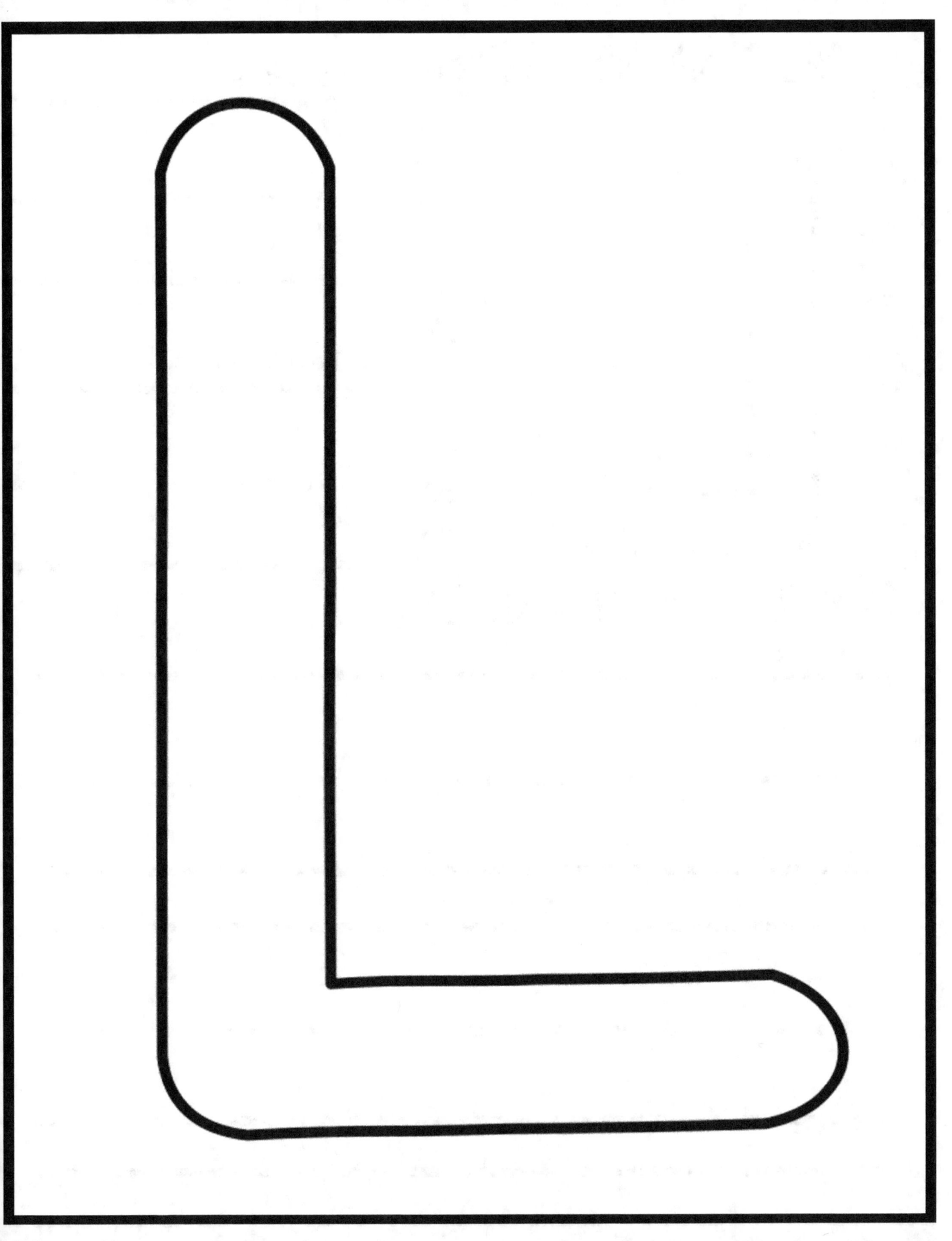

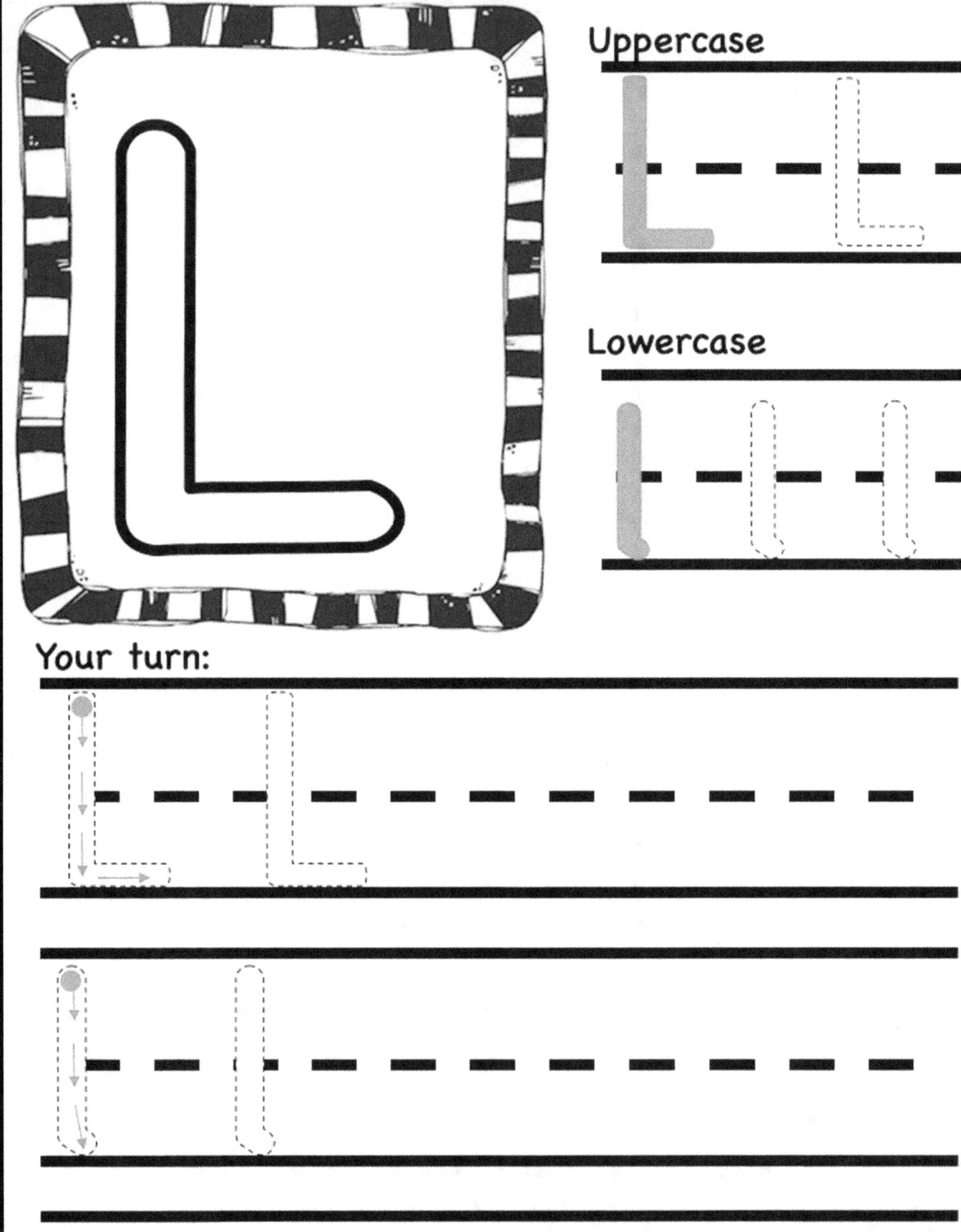

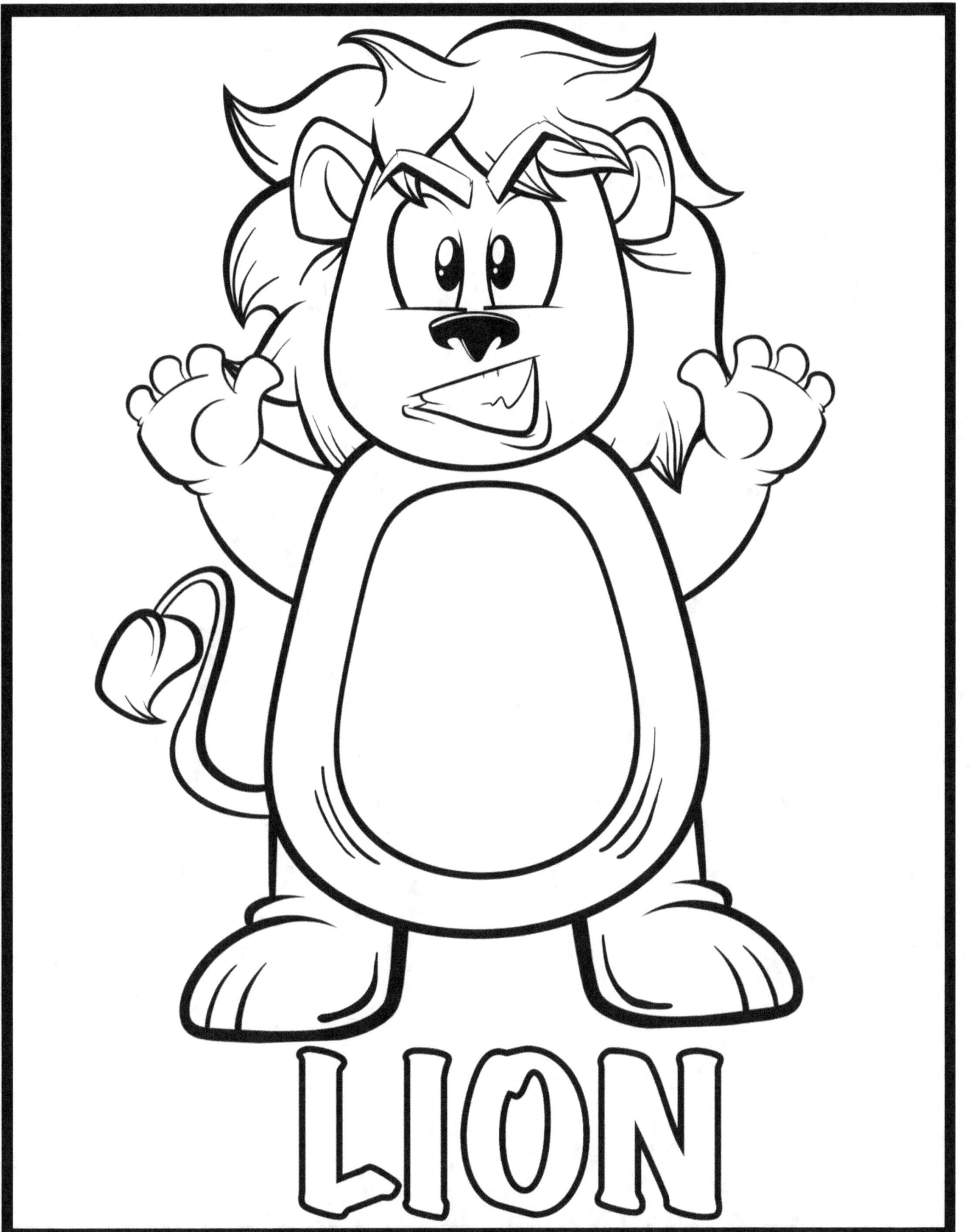

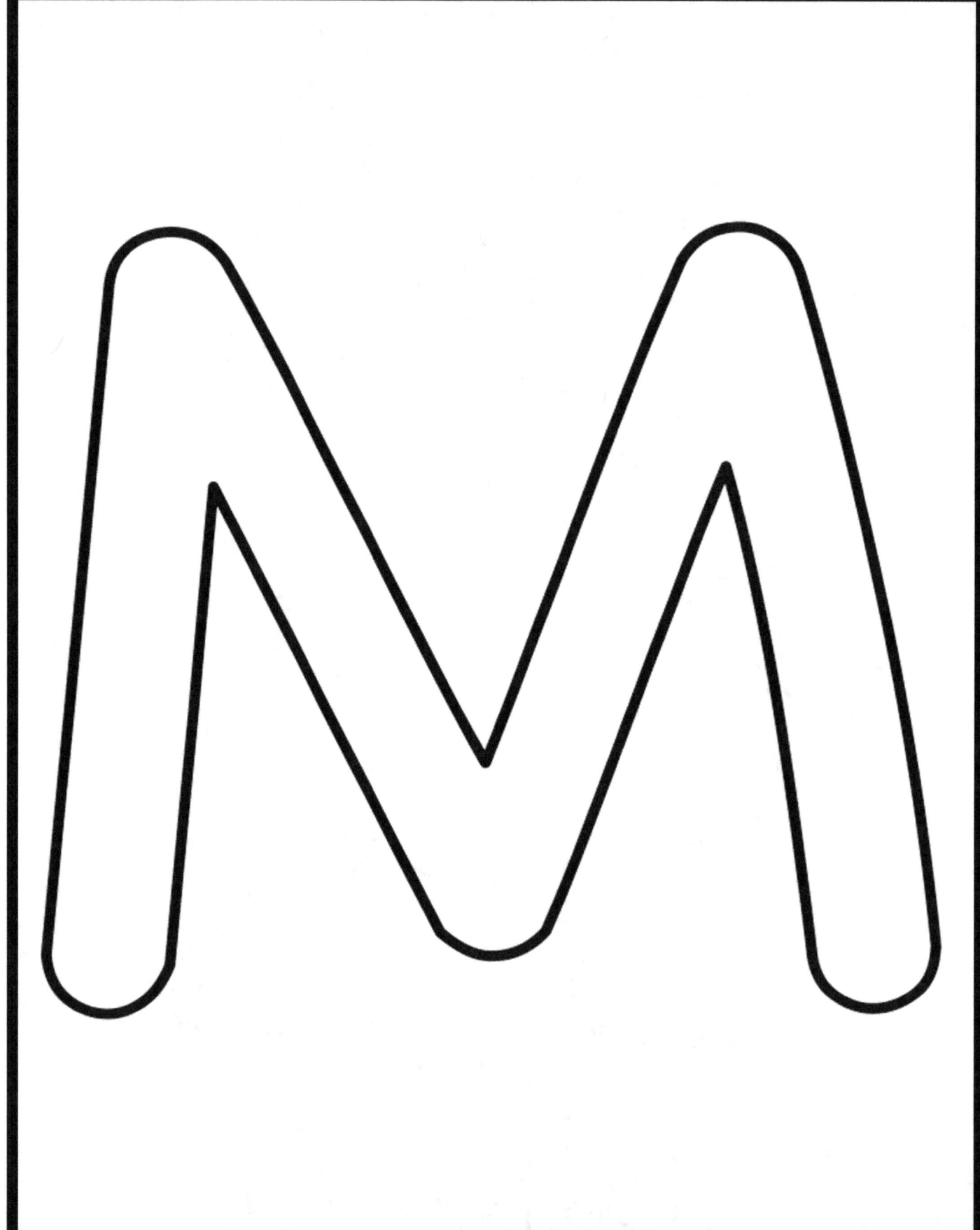

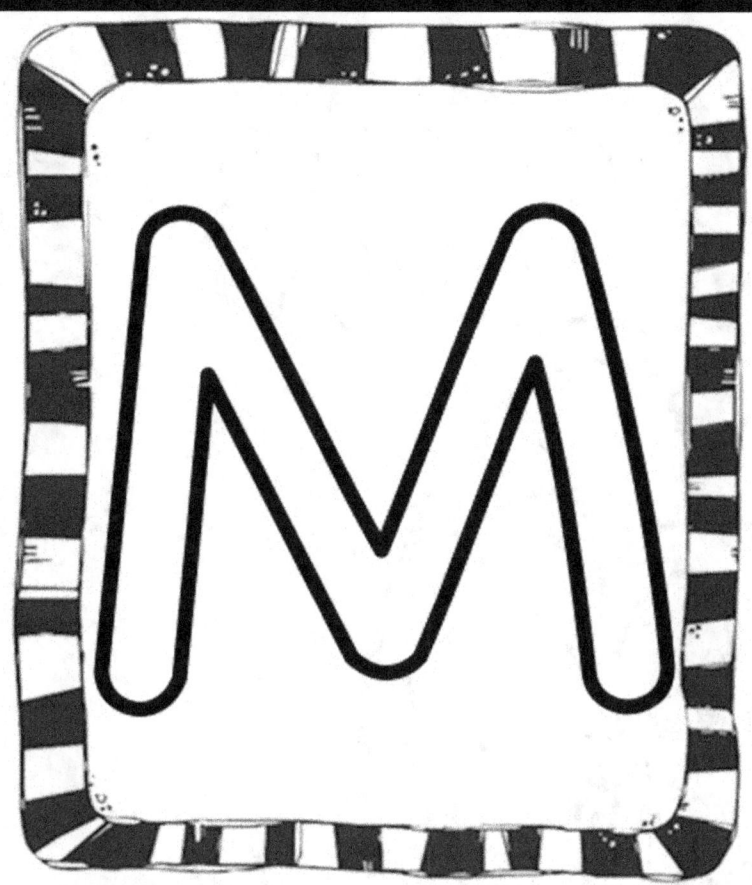

Uppercase

Lowercase

Your turn:

MOUSE

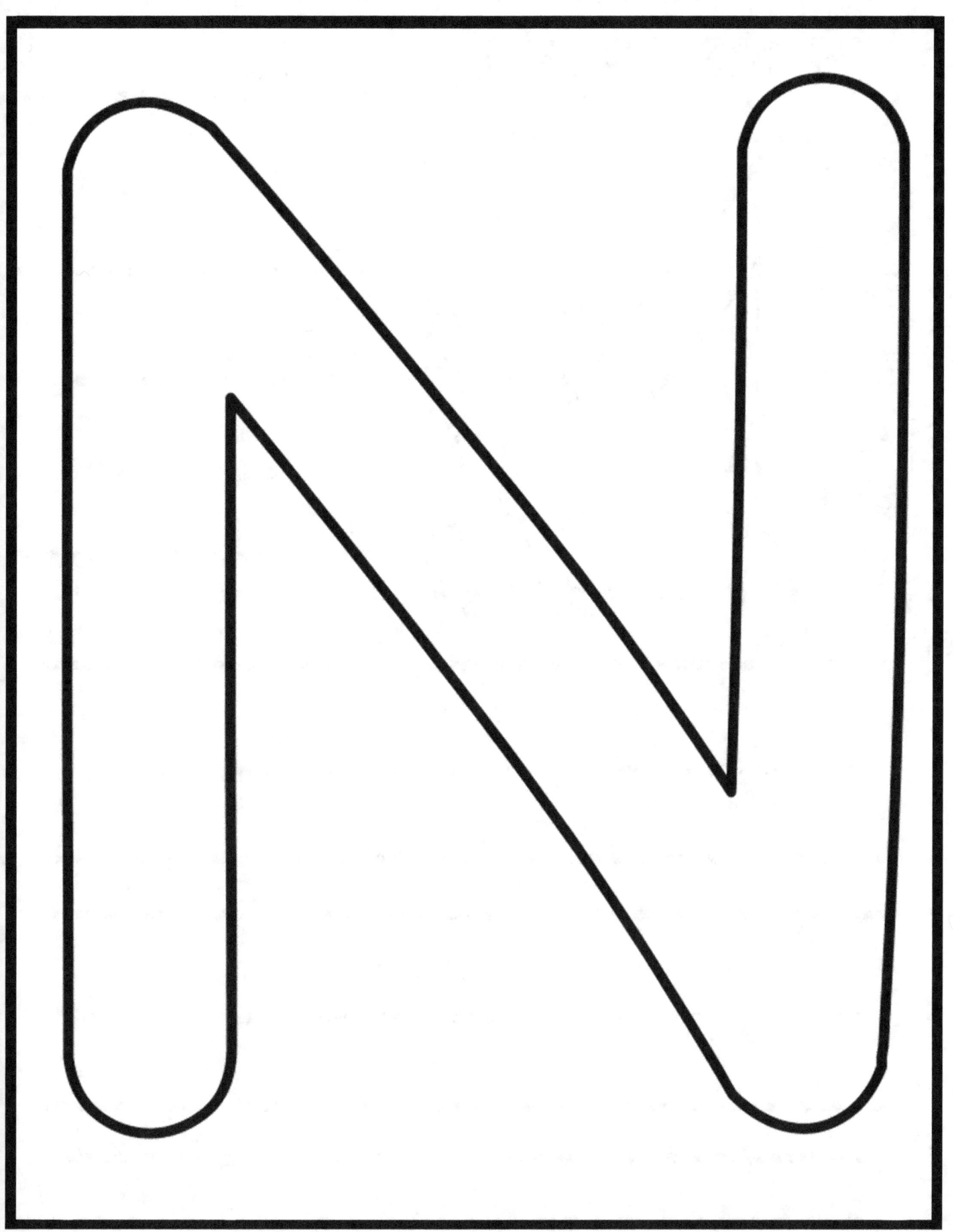

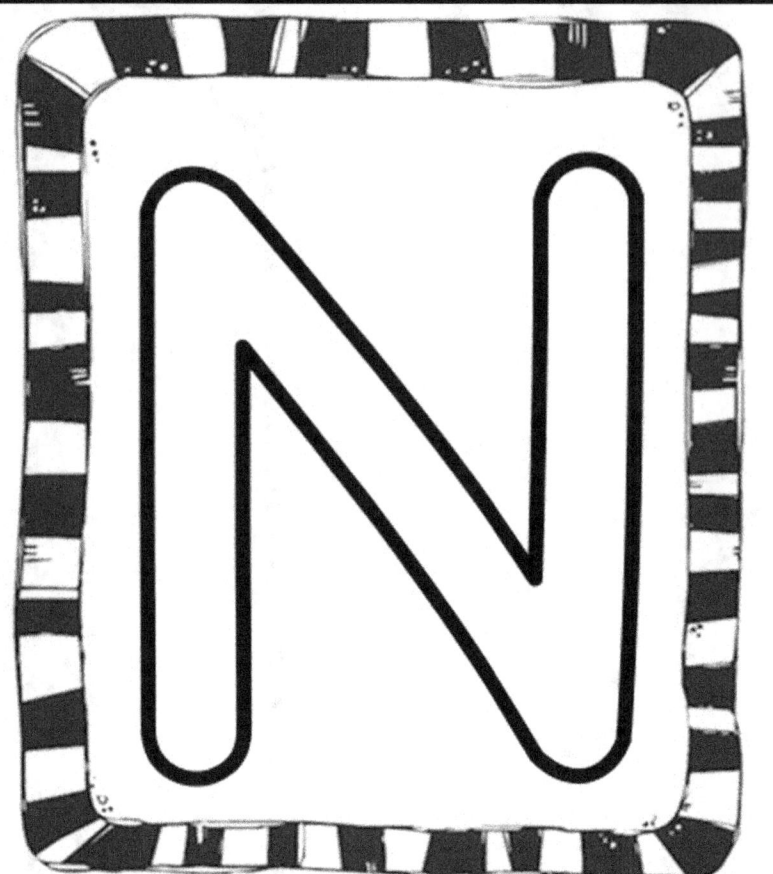

Uppercase

Lowercase

Your turn:

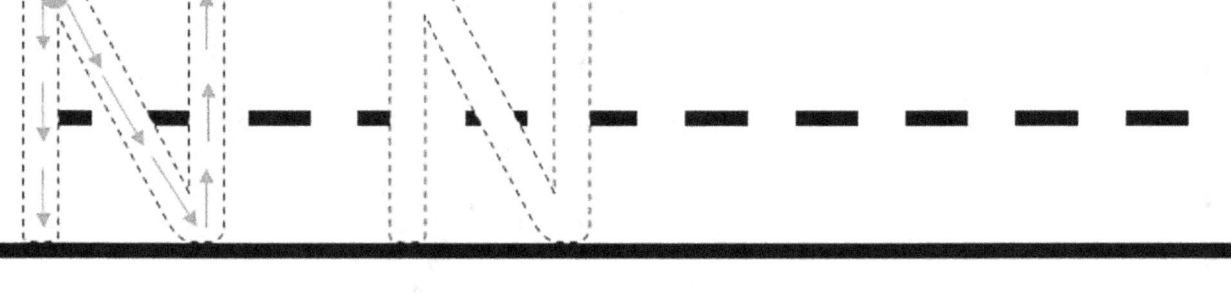

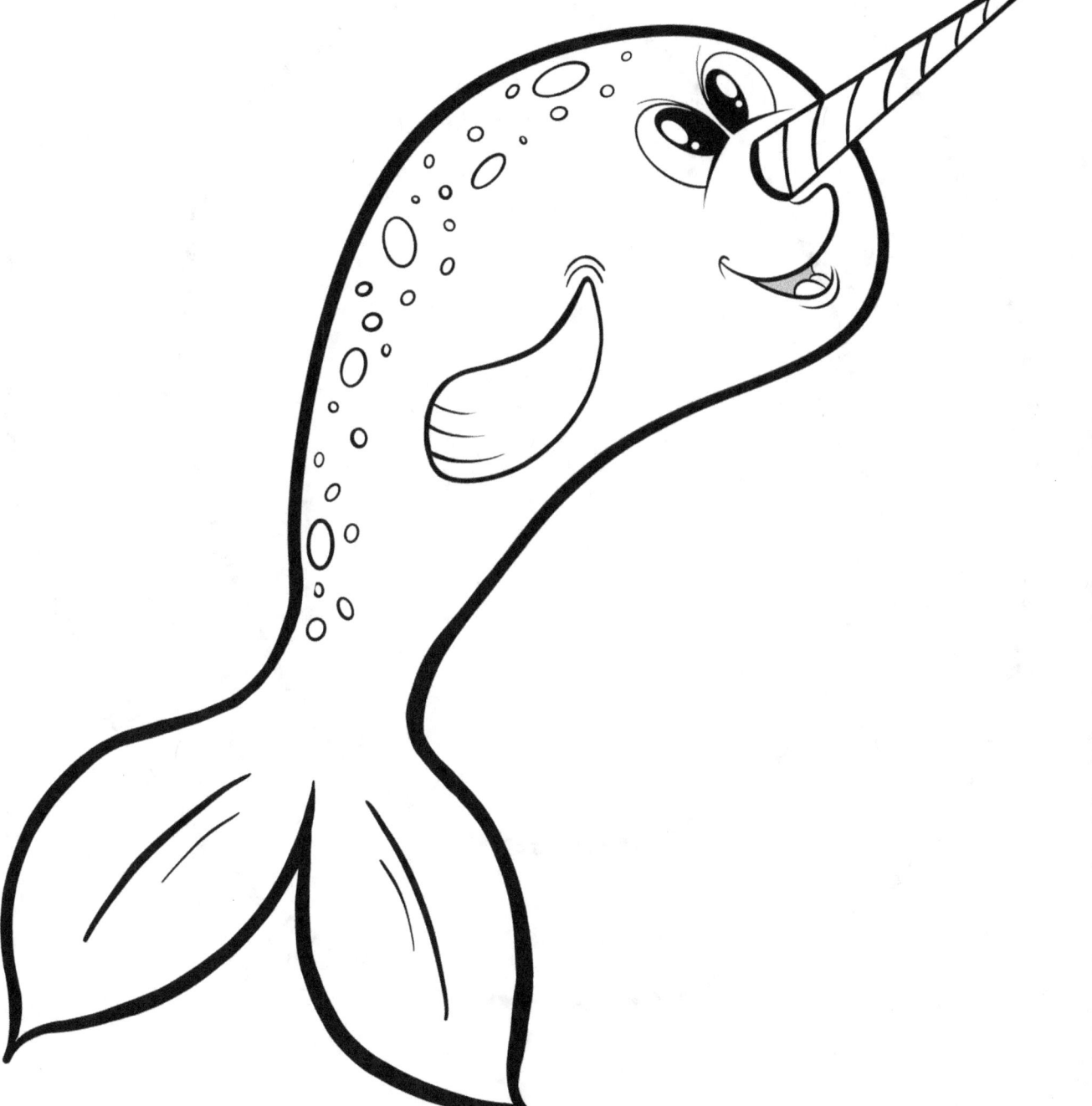

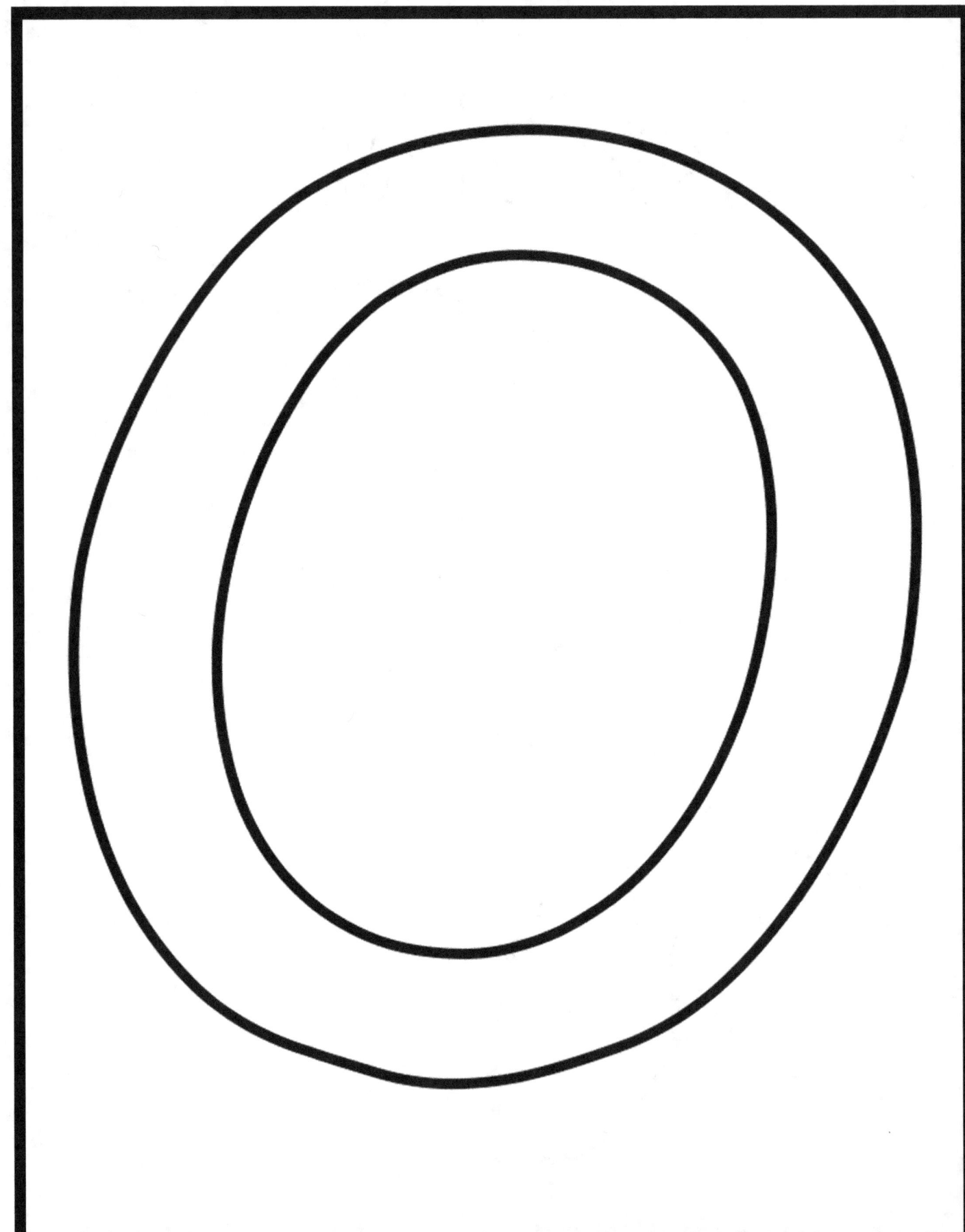

Uppercase

Lowercase

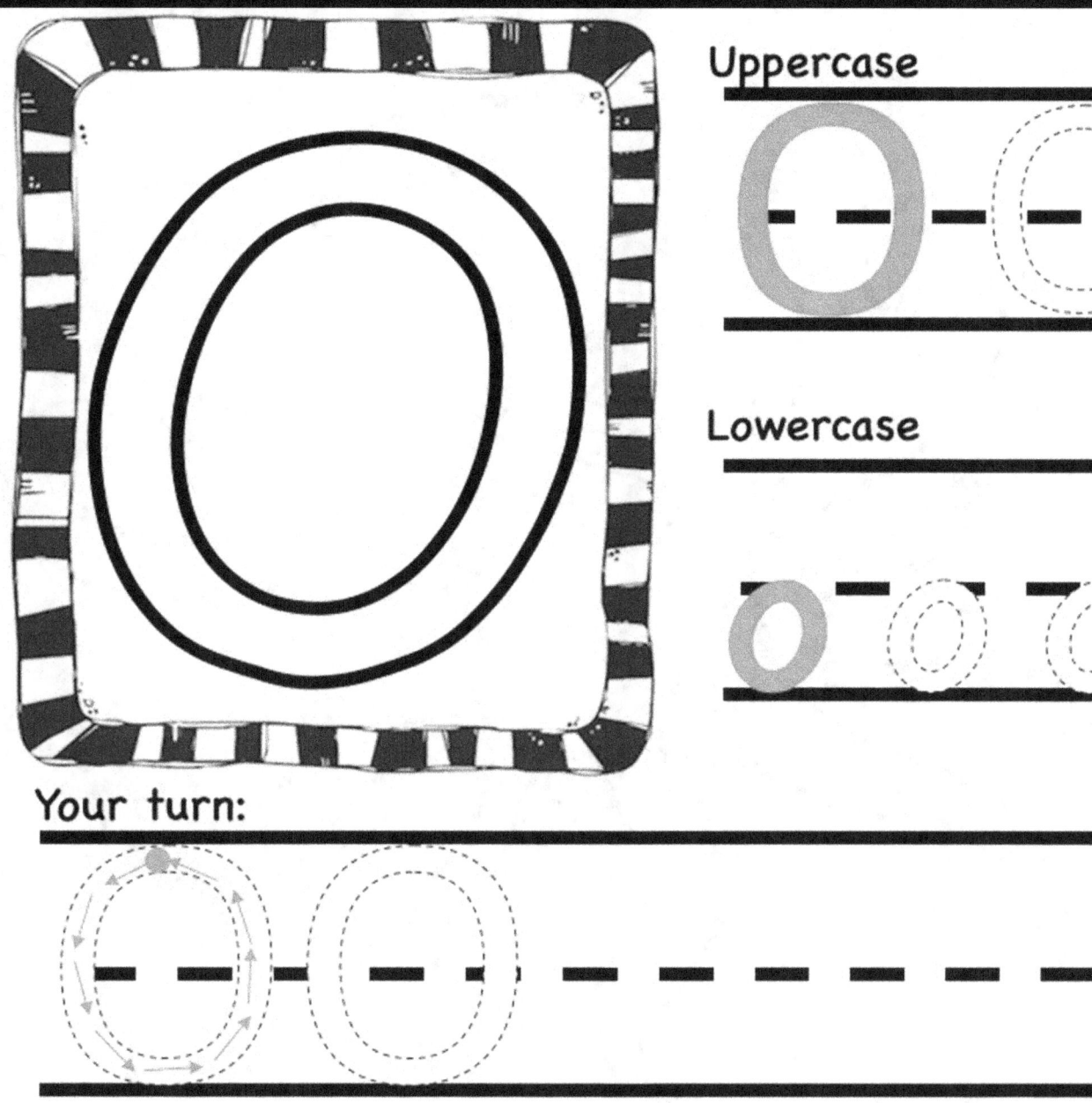

Your turn:

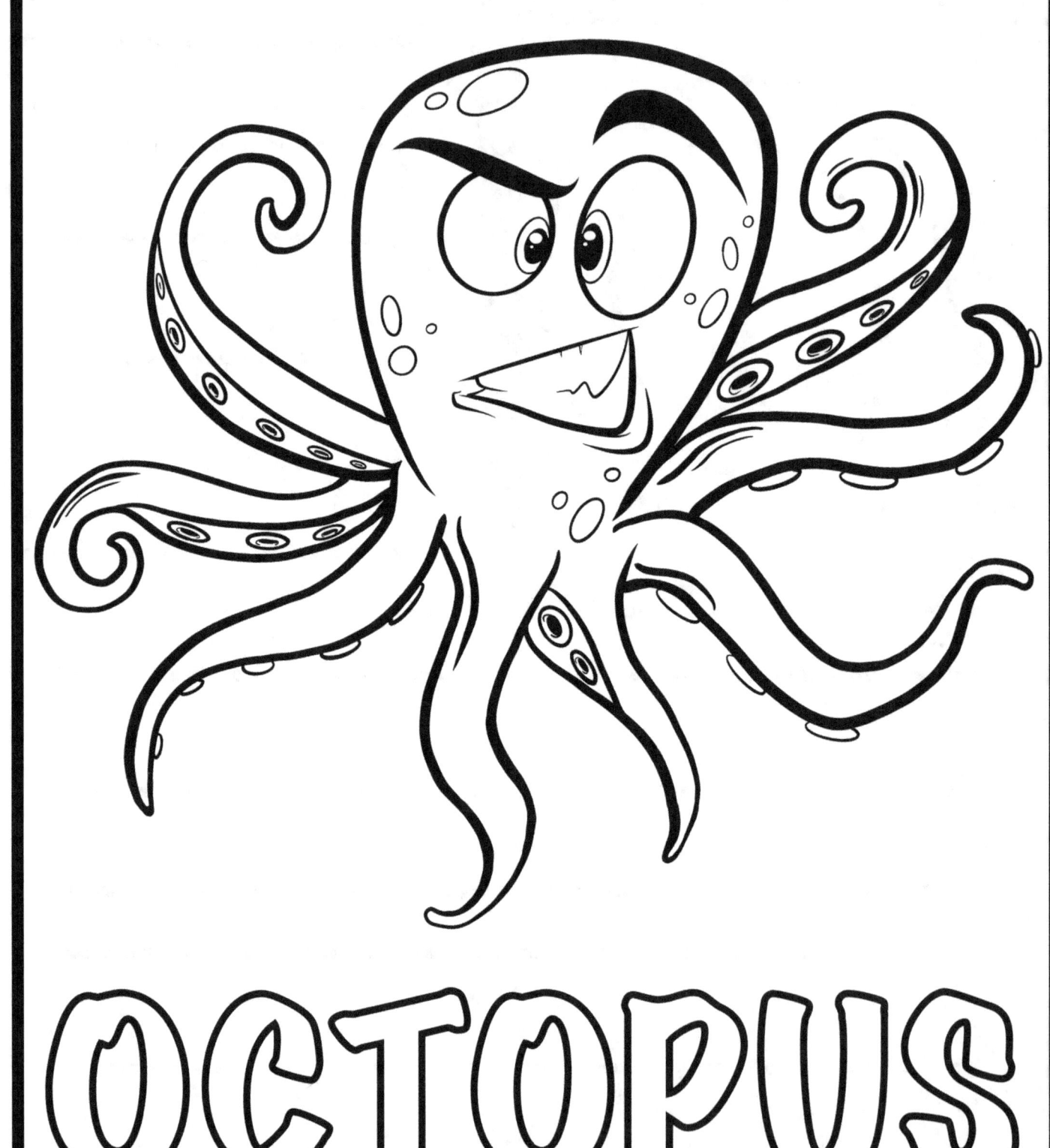

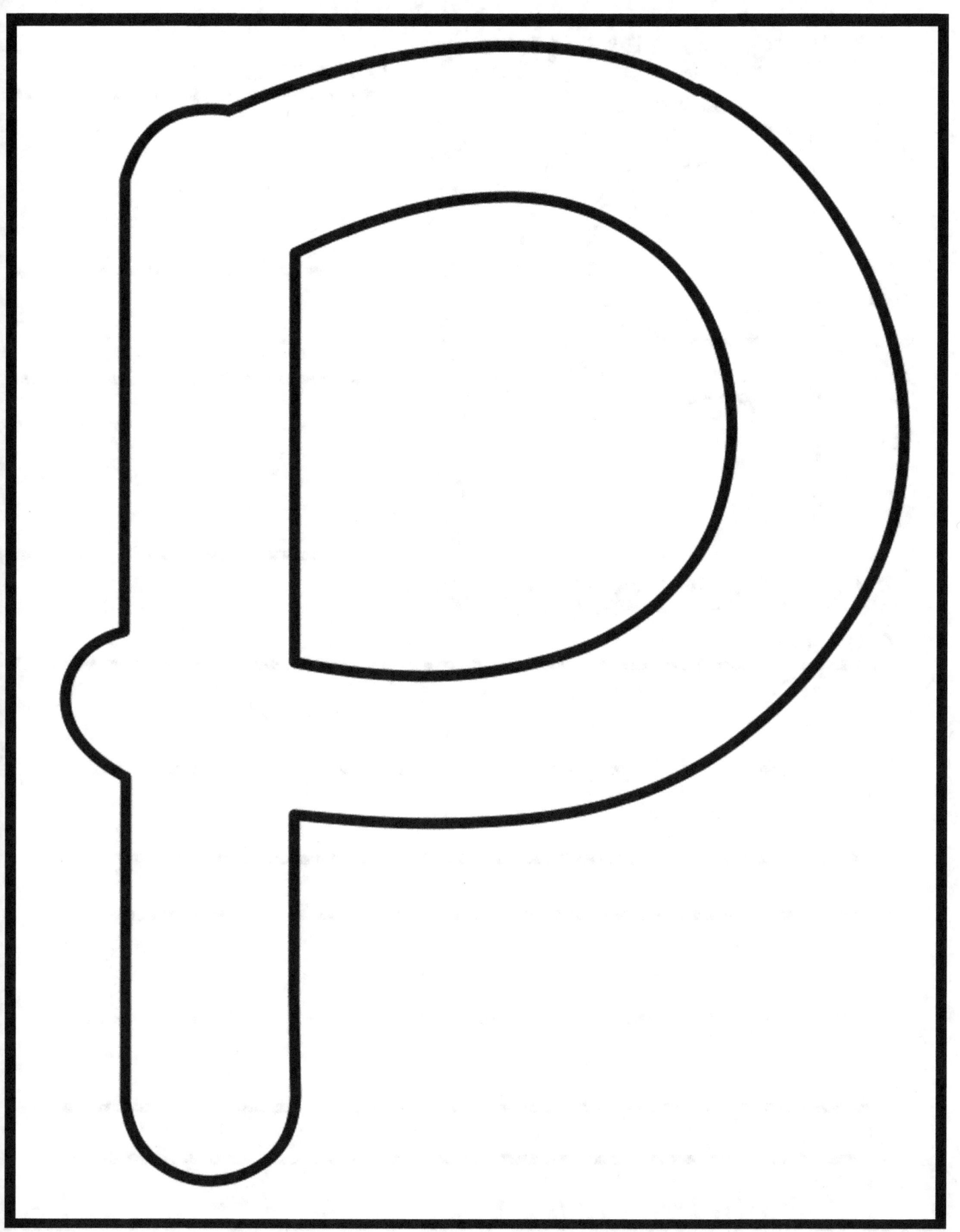

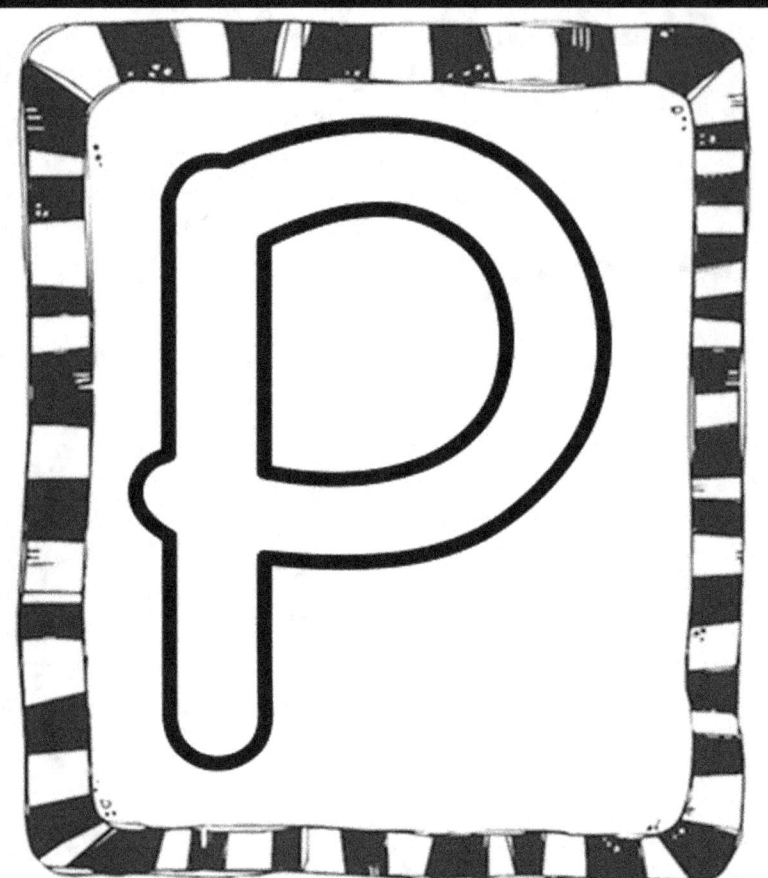

Uppercase

P P

Lowercase

p p p

Your turn:

P P

p p

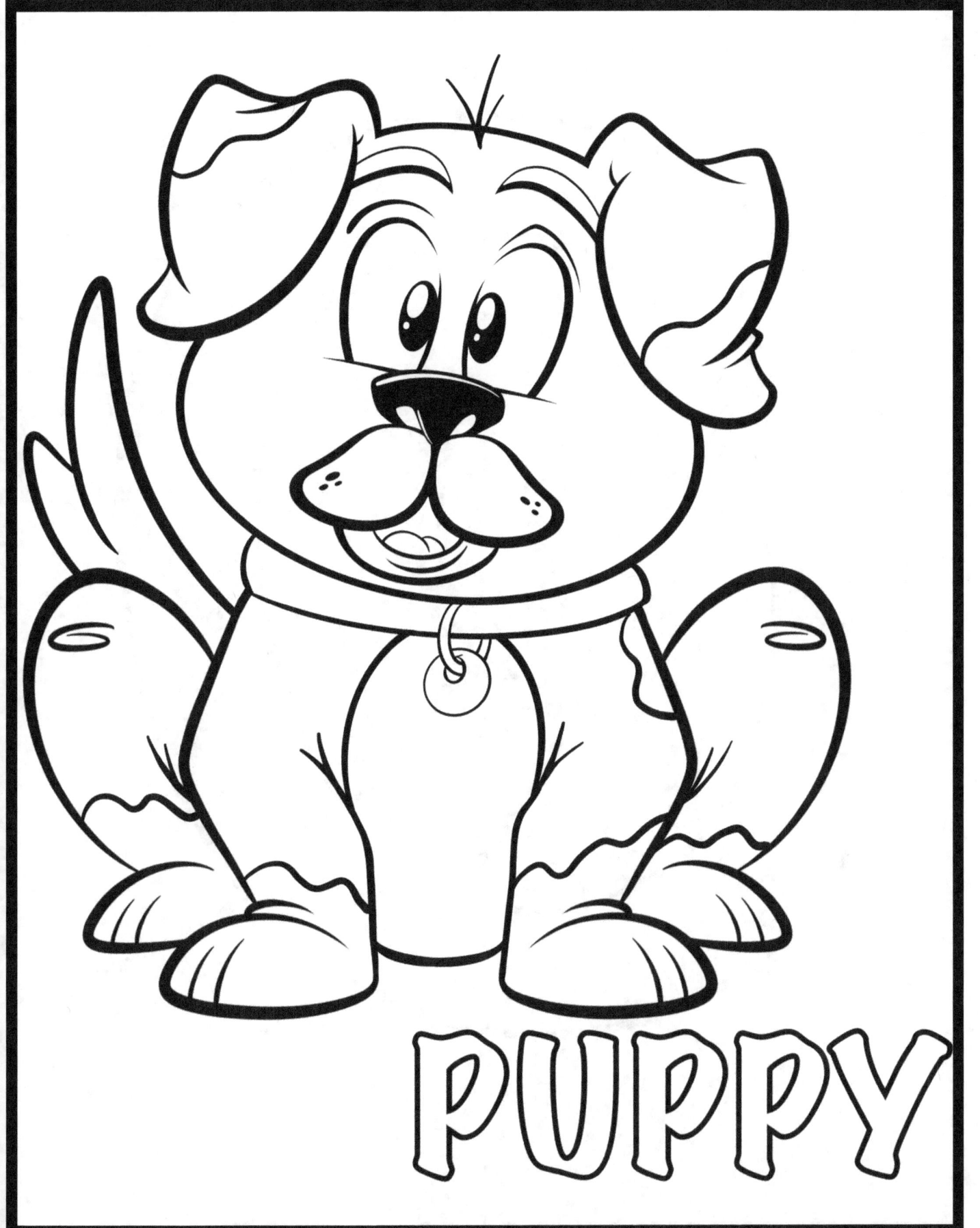

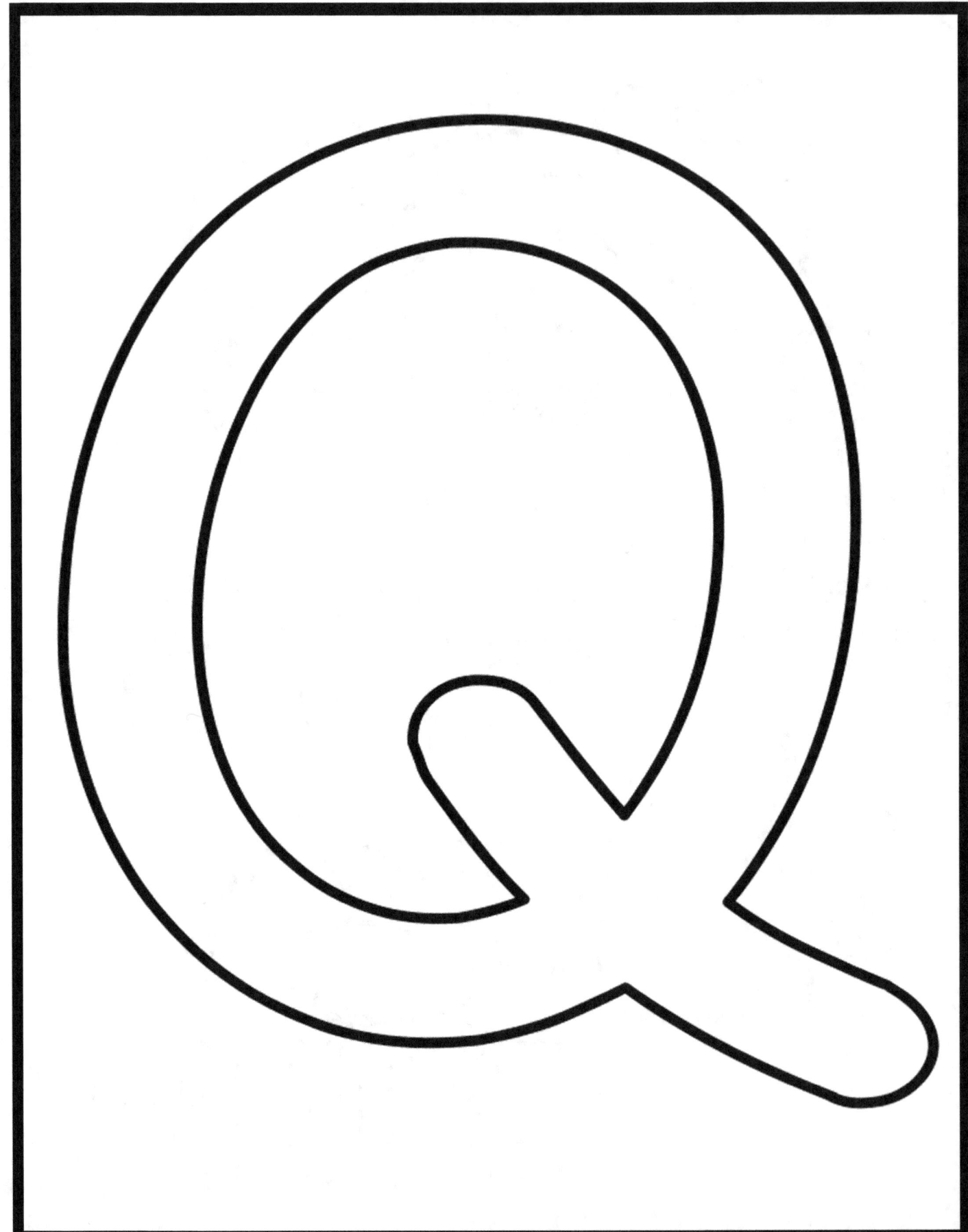

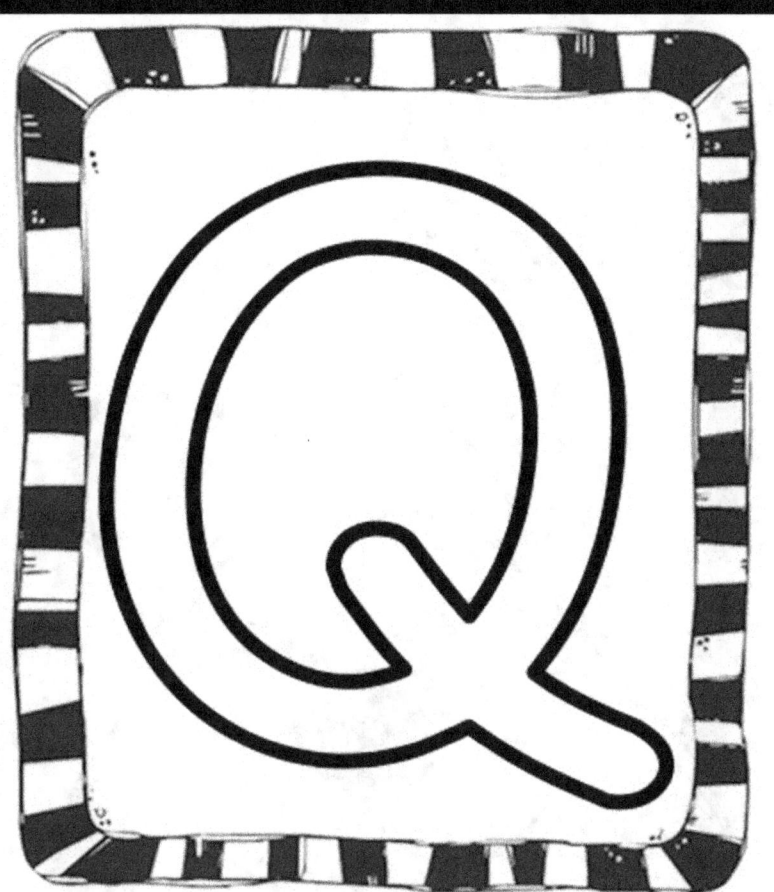

Uppercase

Lowercase

Your turn:

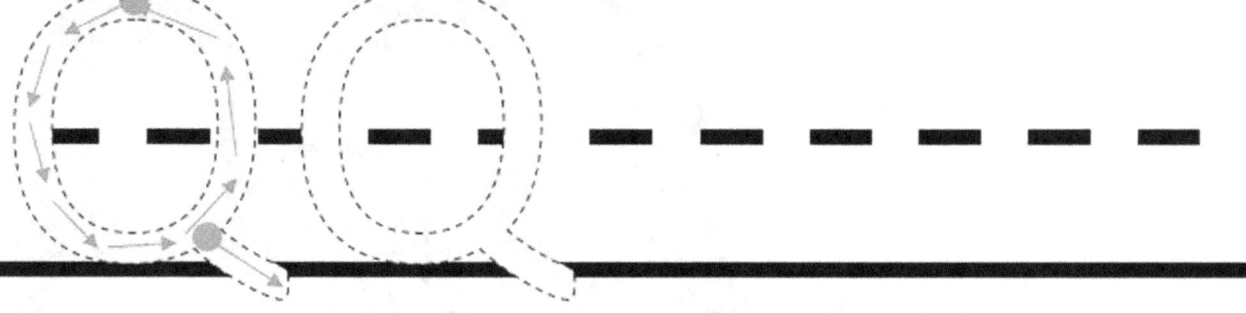

QUOKKA

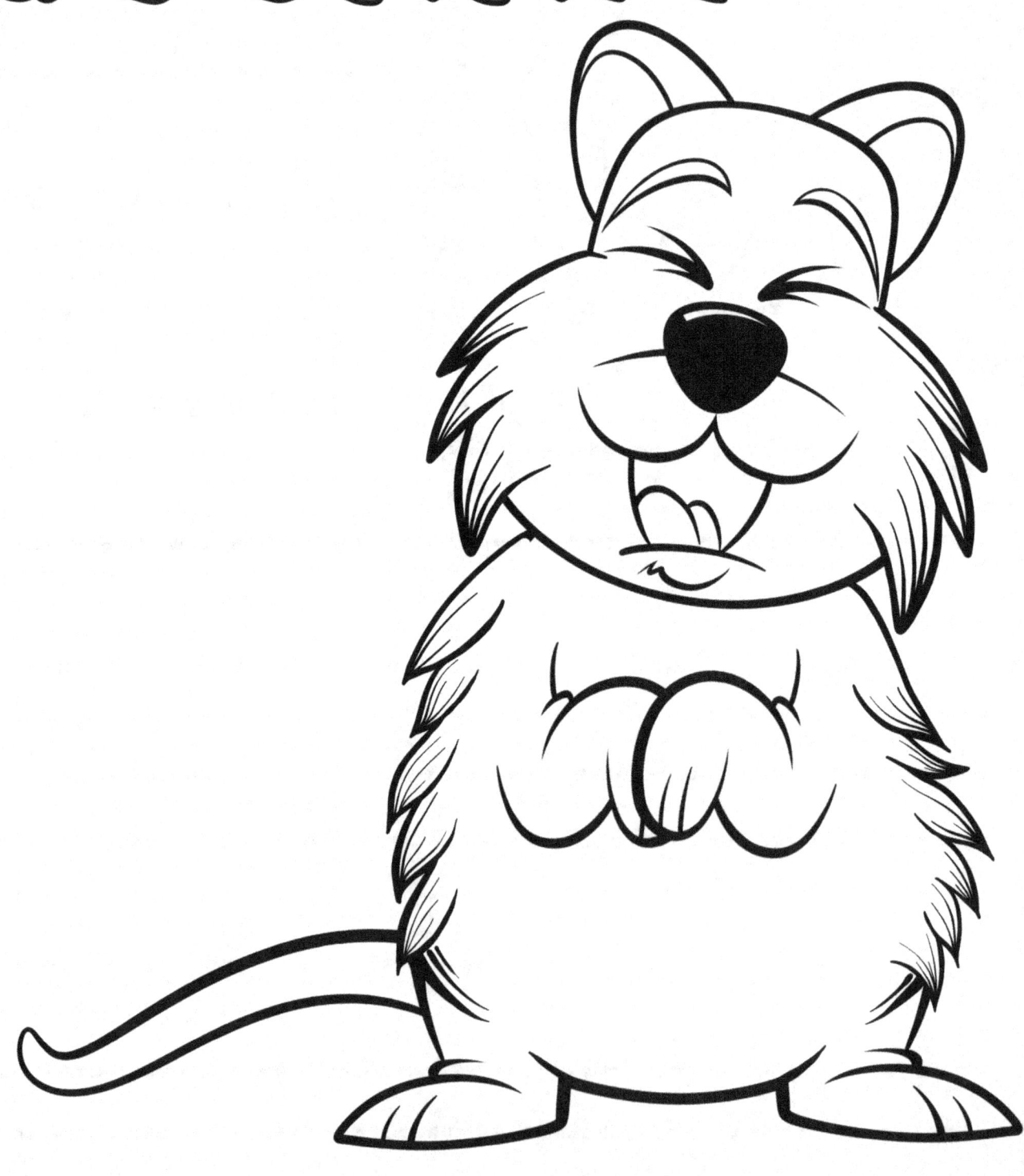

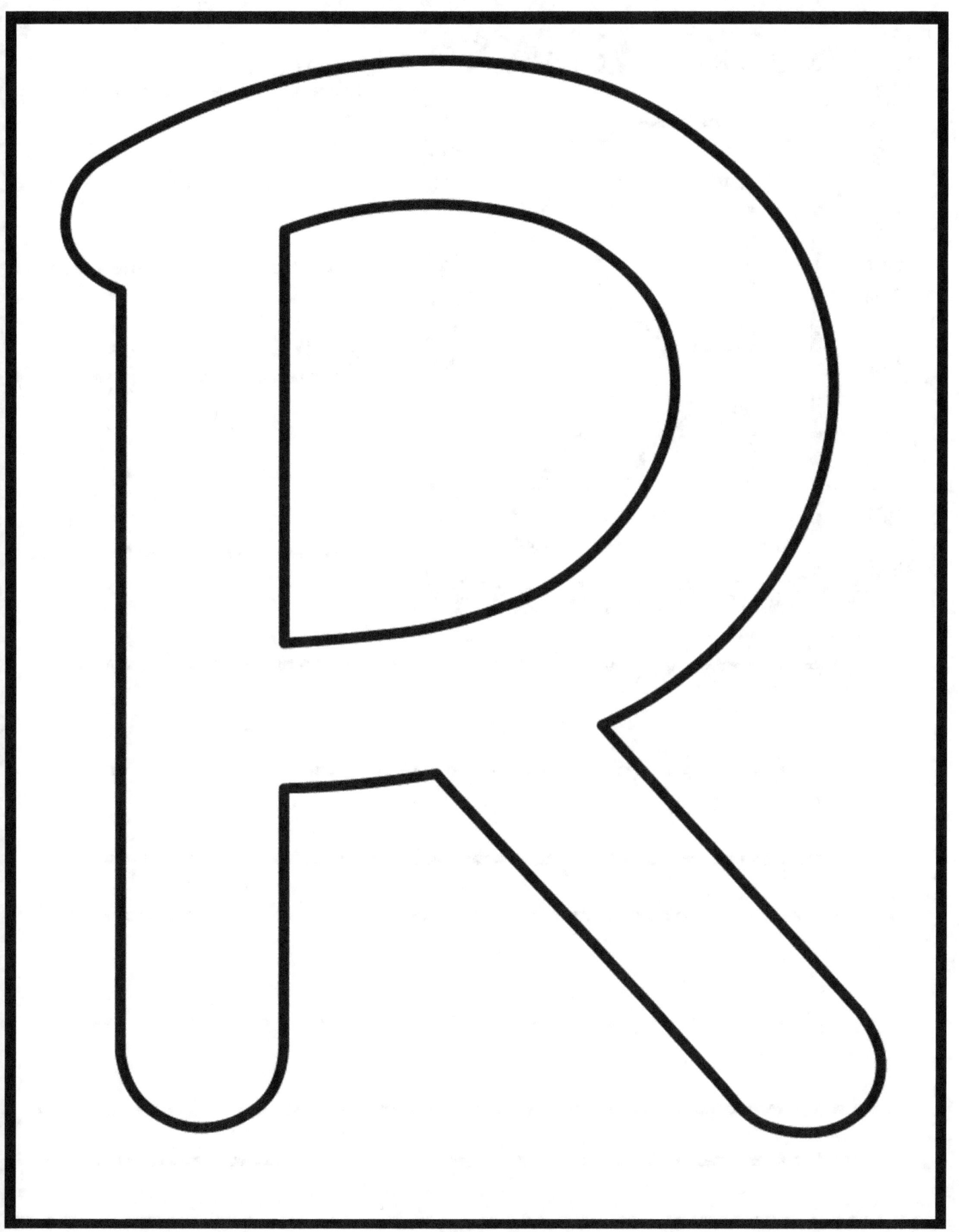

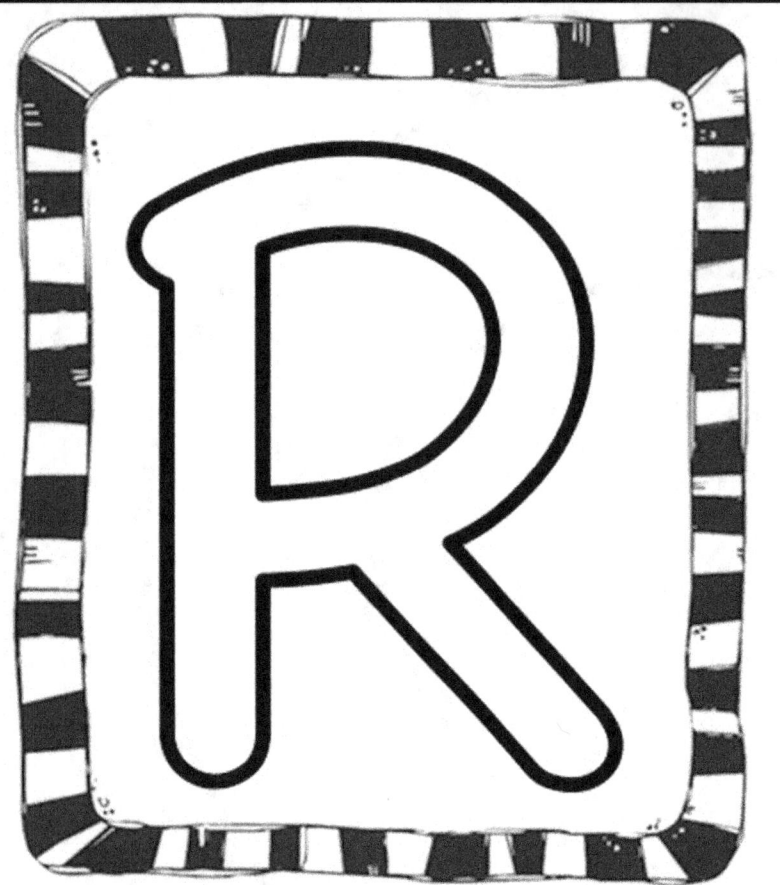

Uppercase

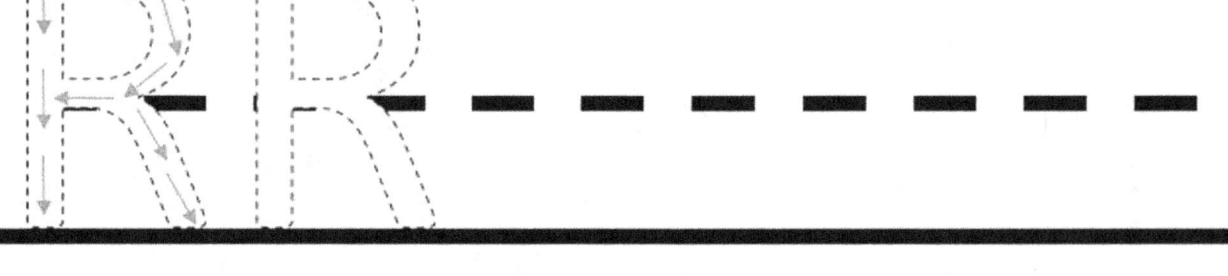

Lowercase

Your turn:

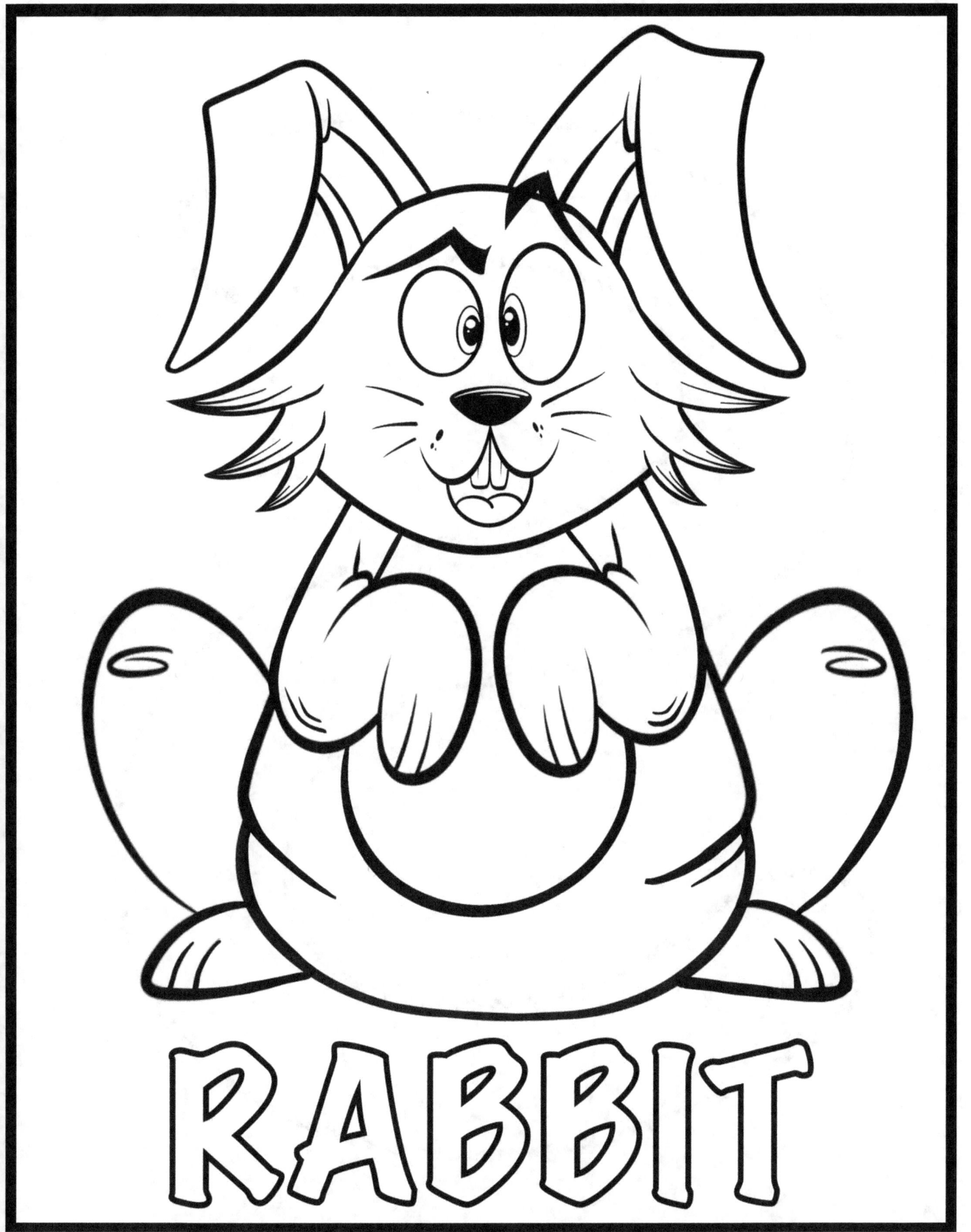

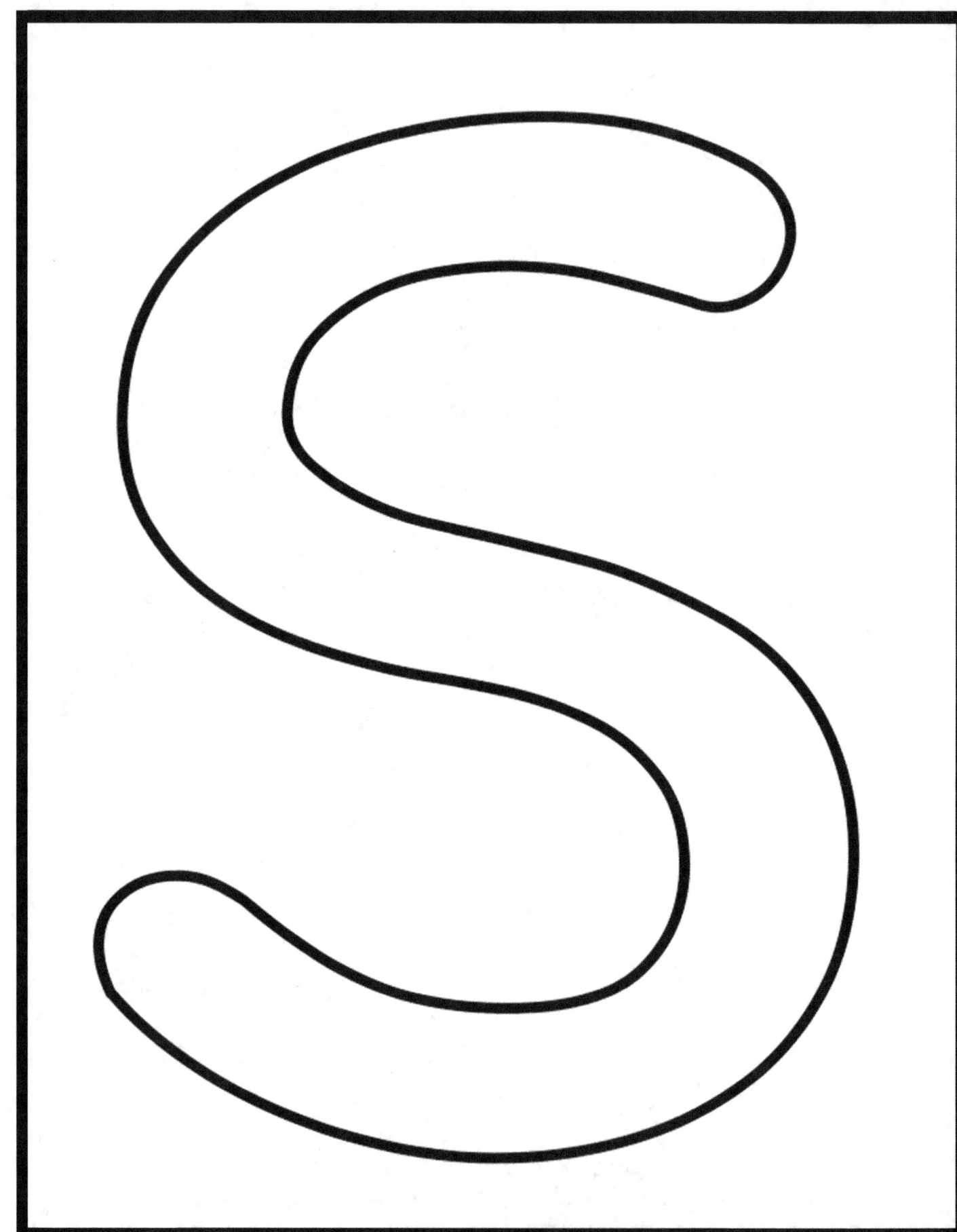

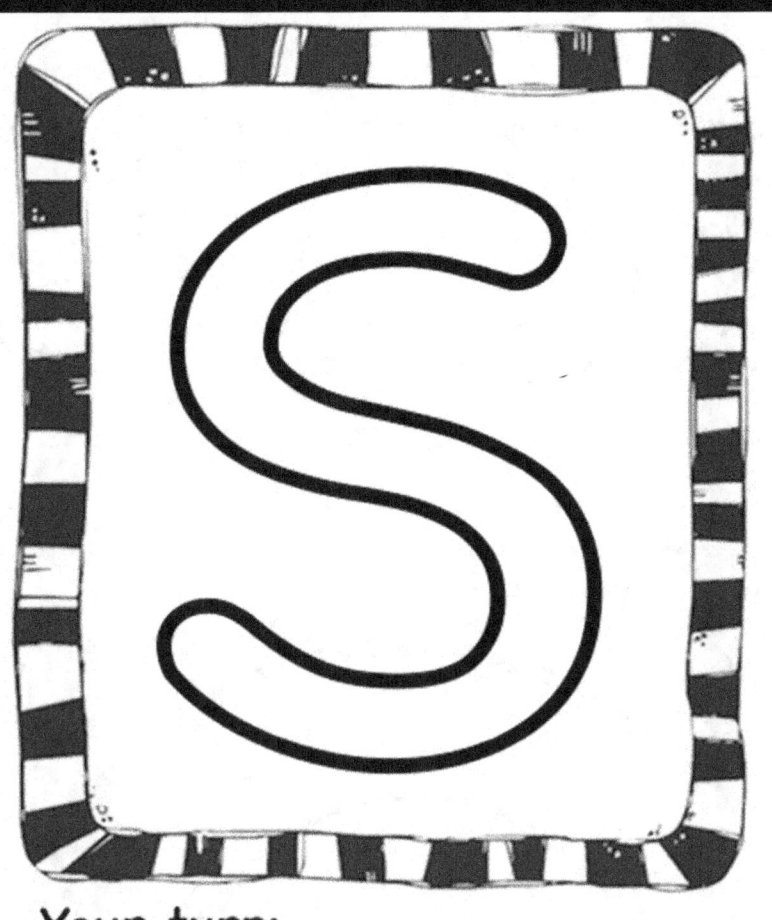

Uppercase

S S S

Lowercase

s s s

Your turn:

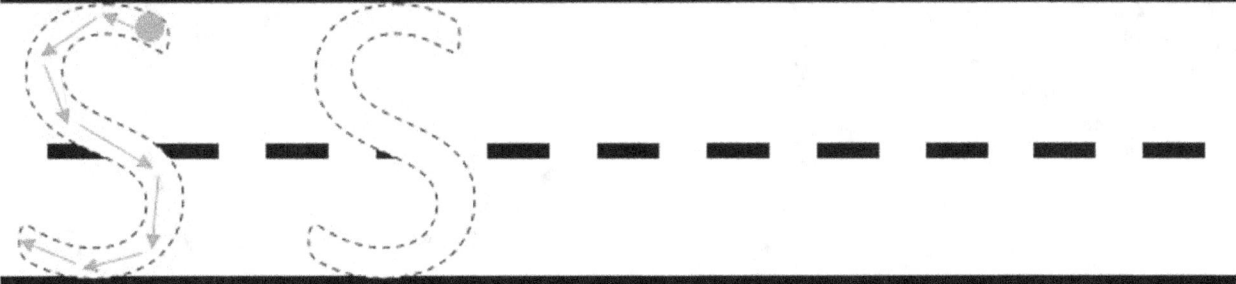

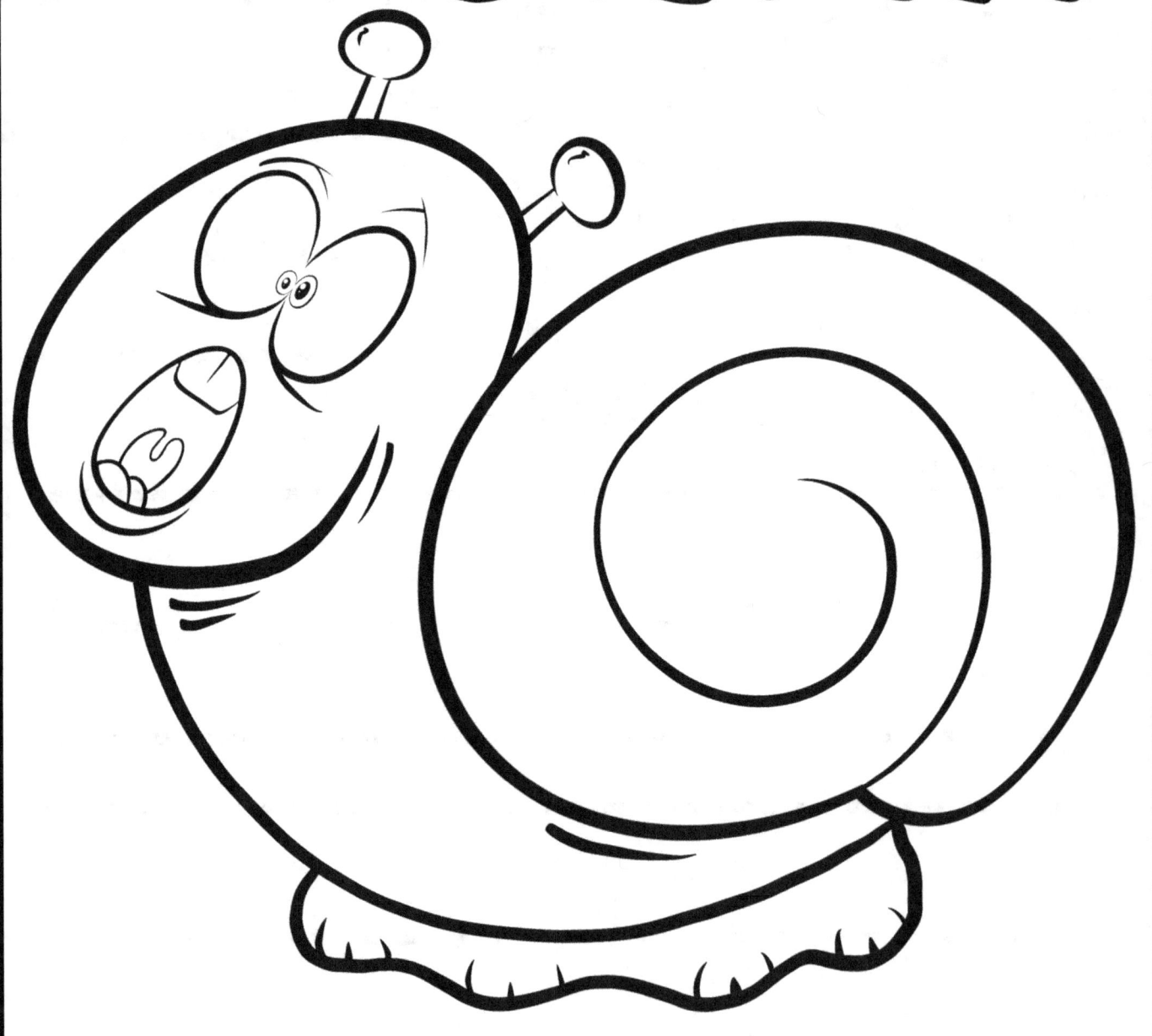

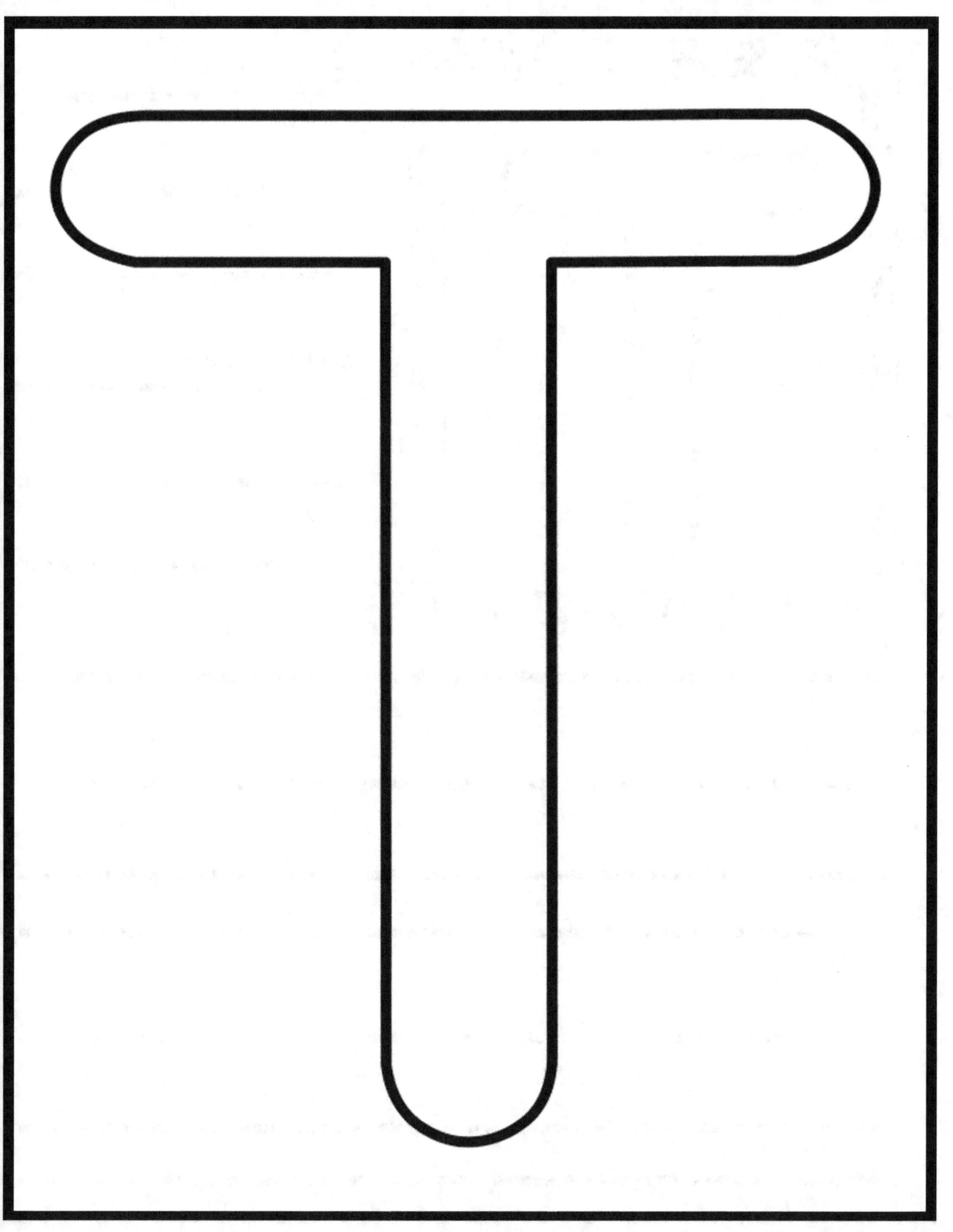

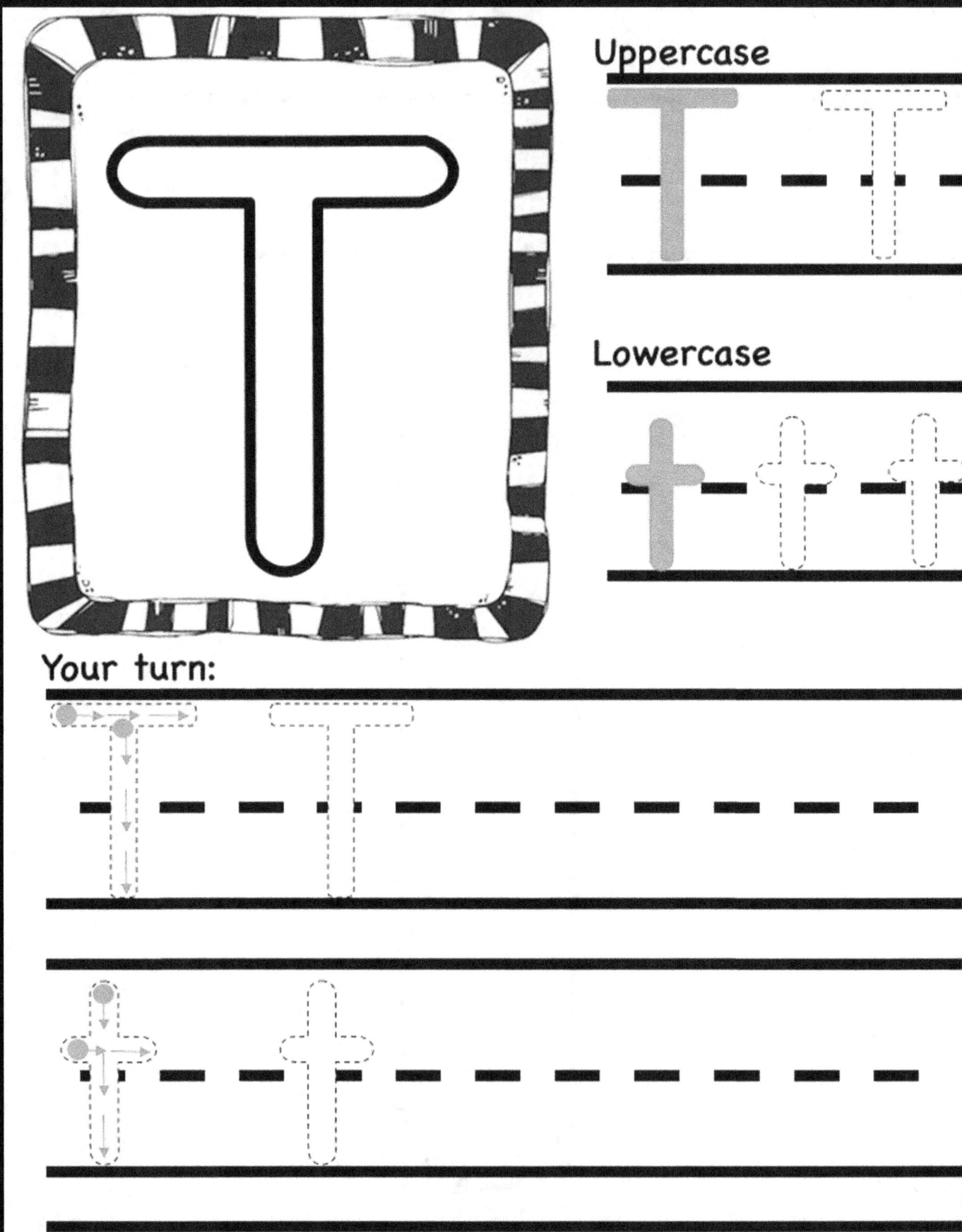

TURTLE

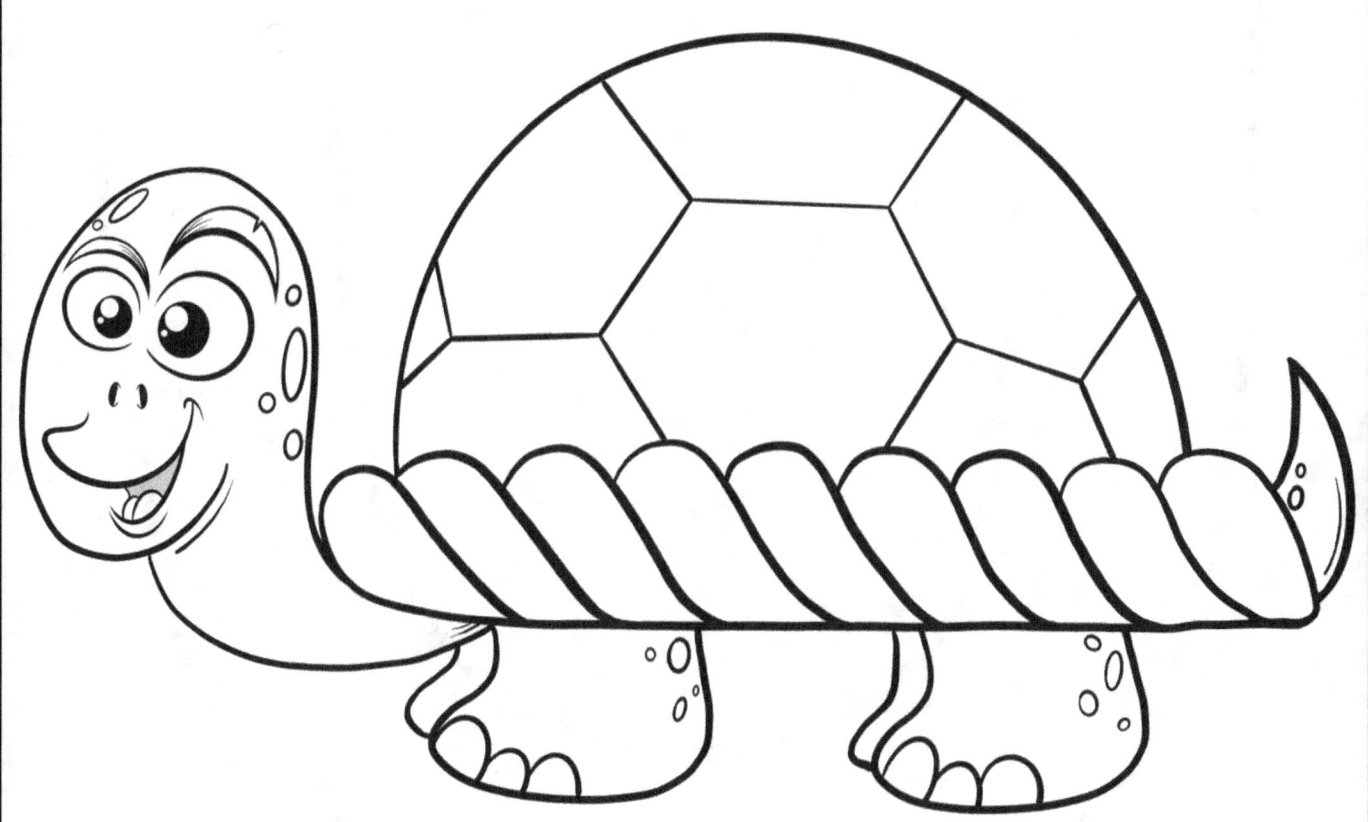

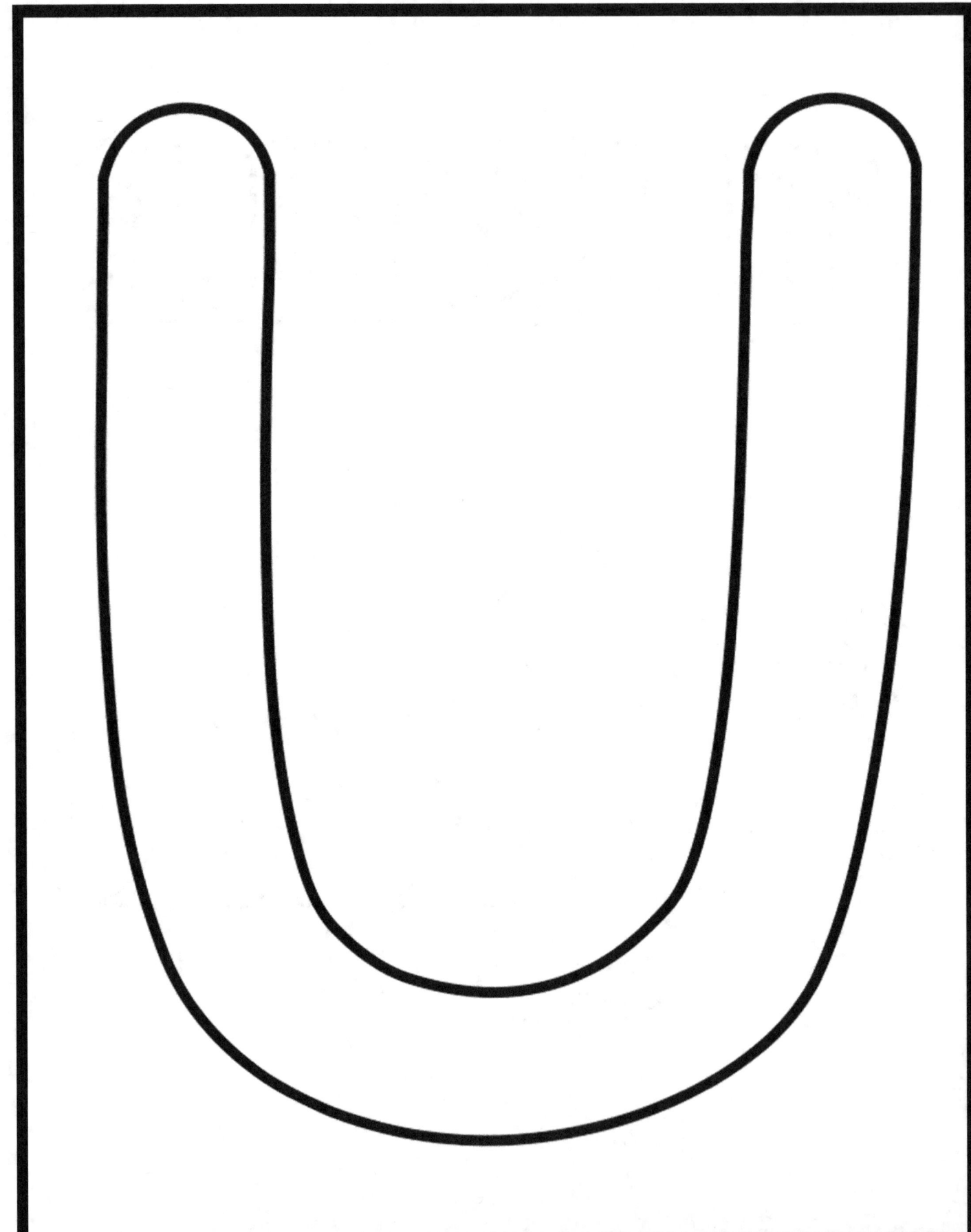

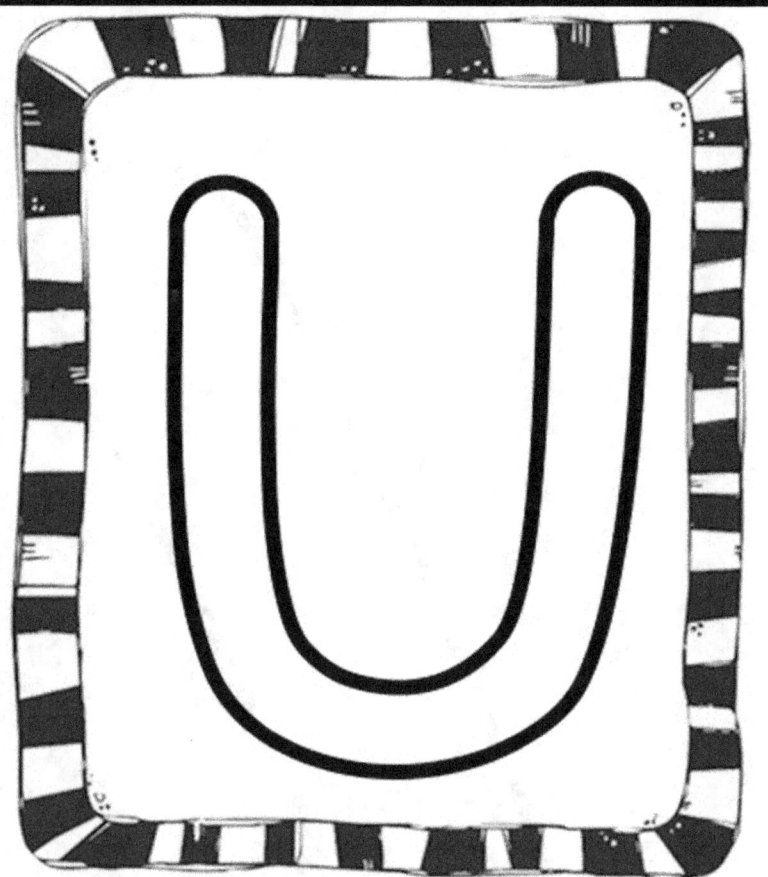

Uppercase

Lowercase

Your turn:

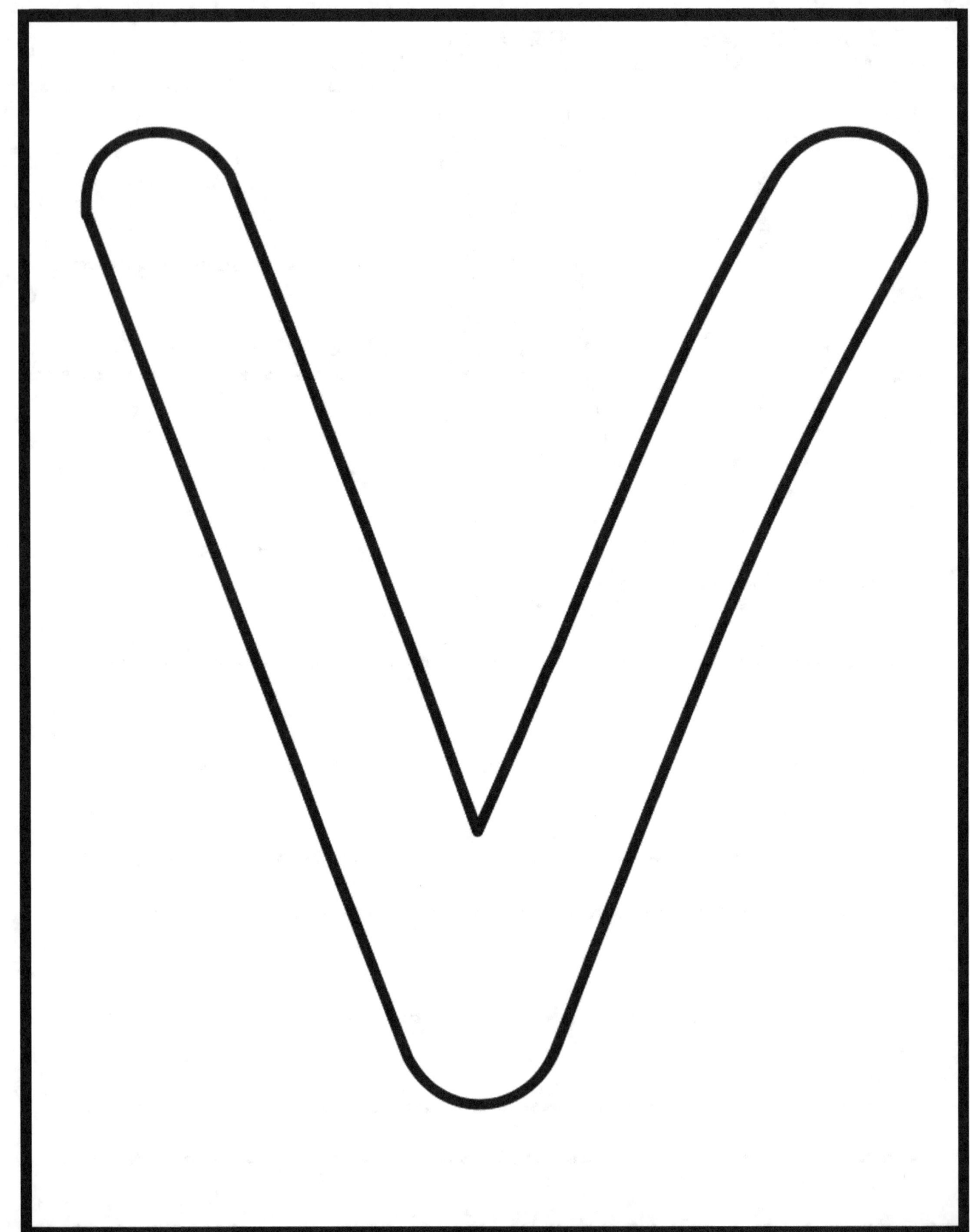

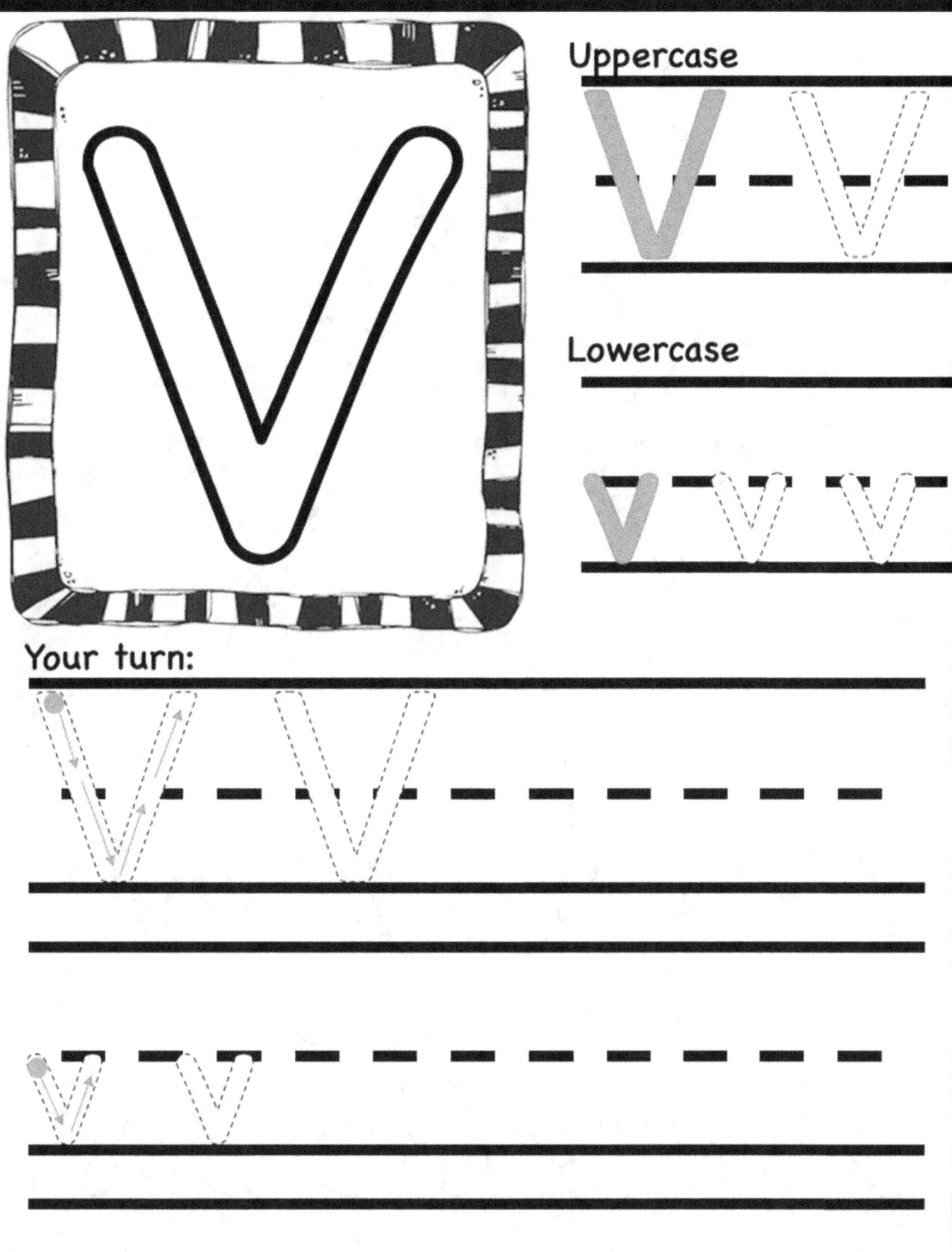

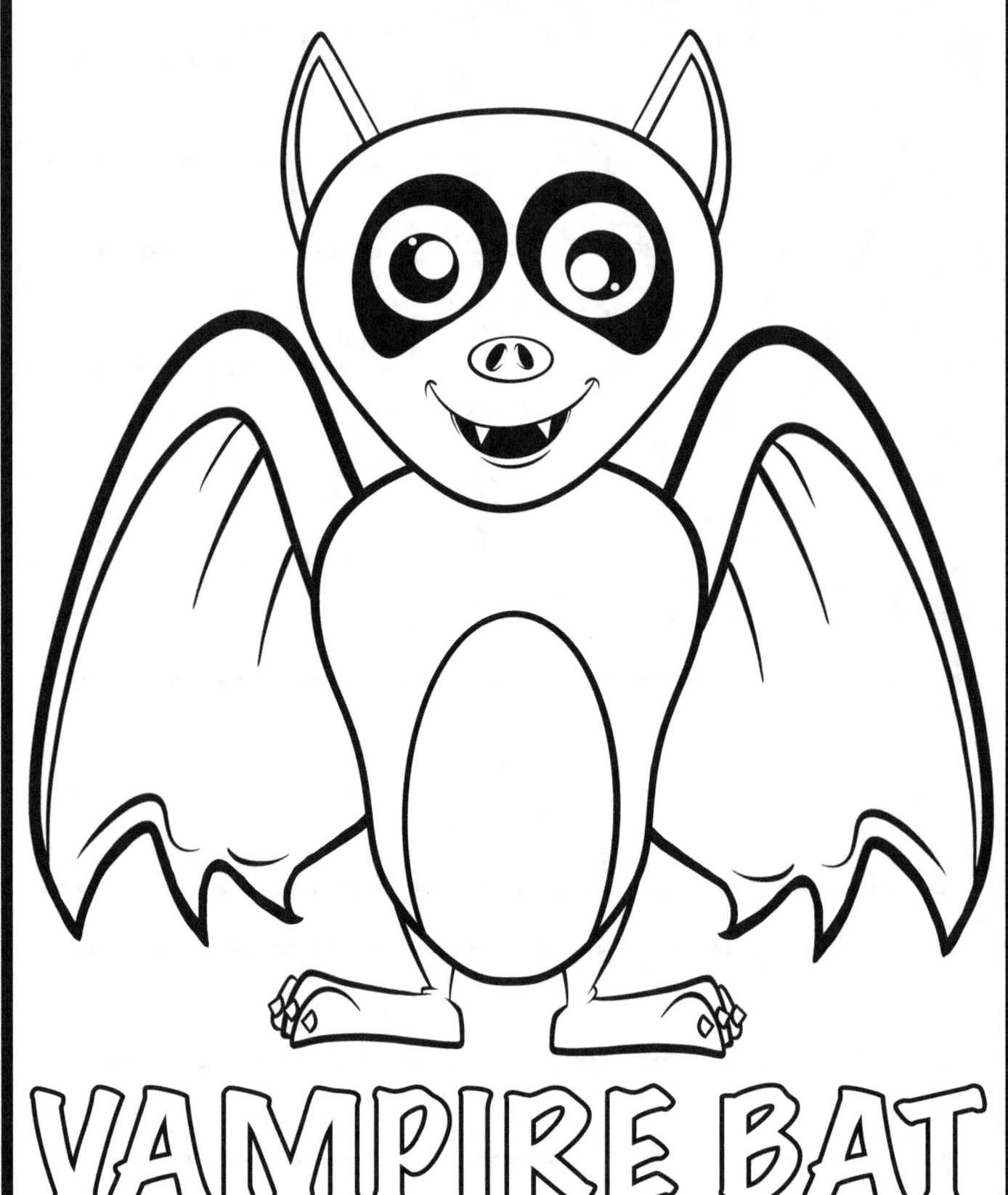

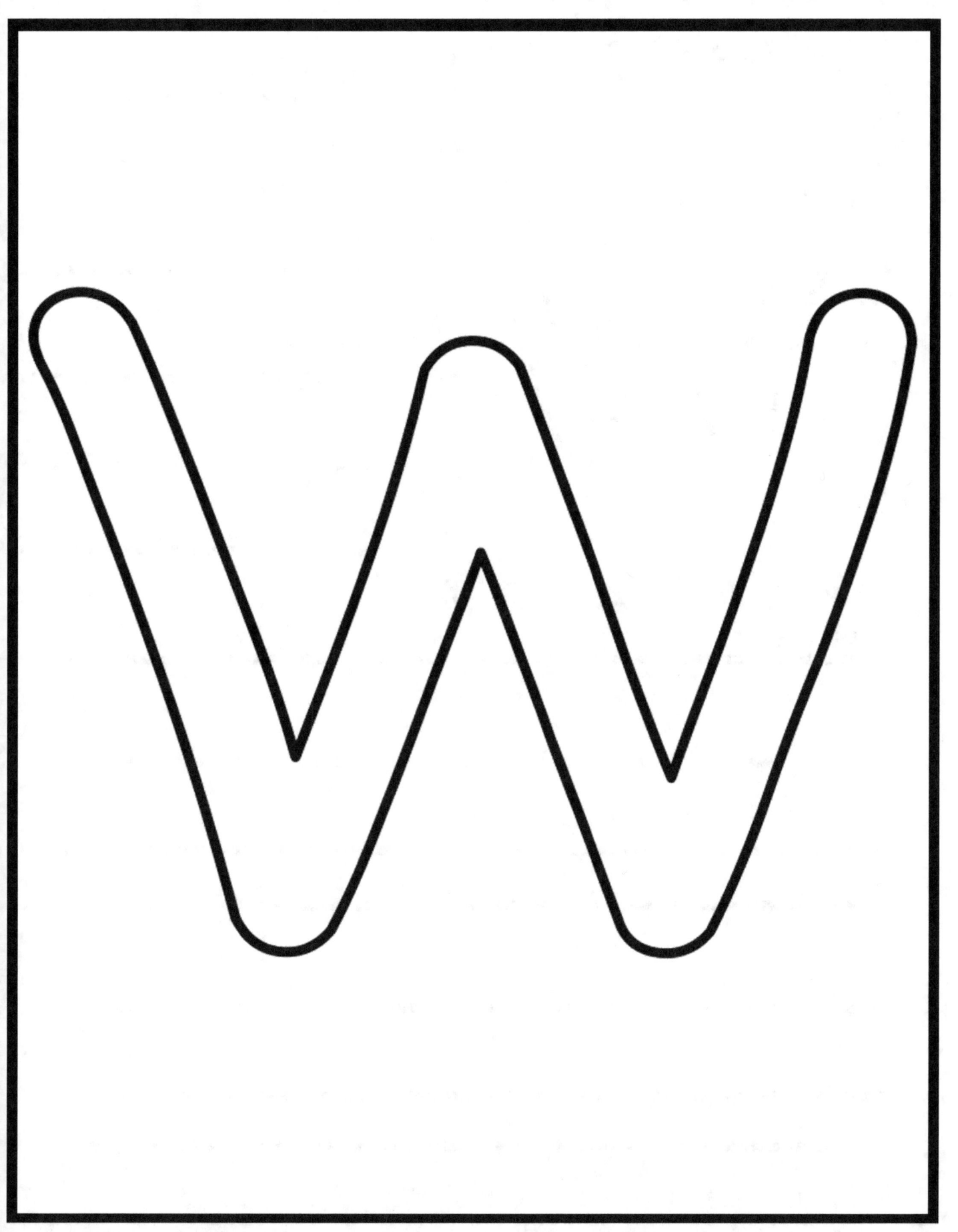

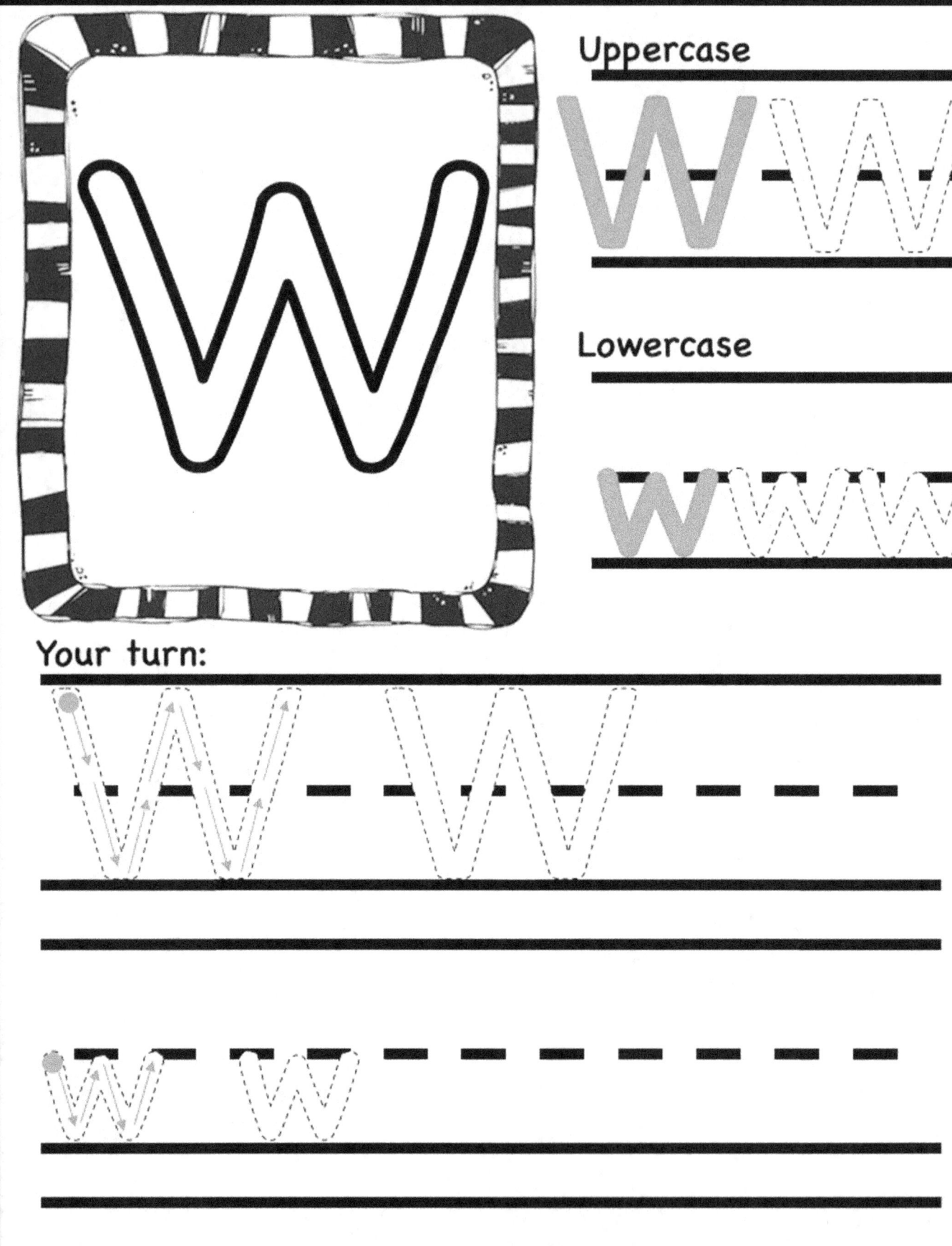

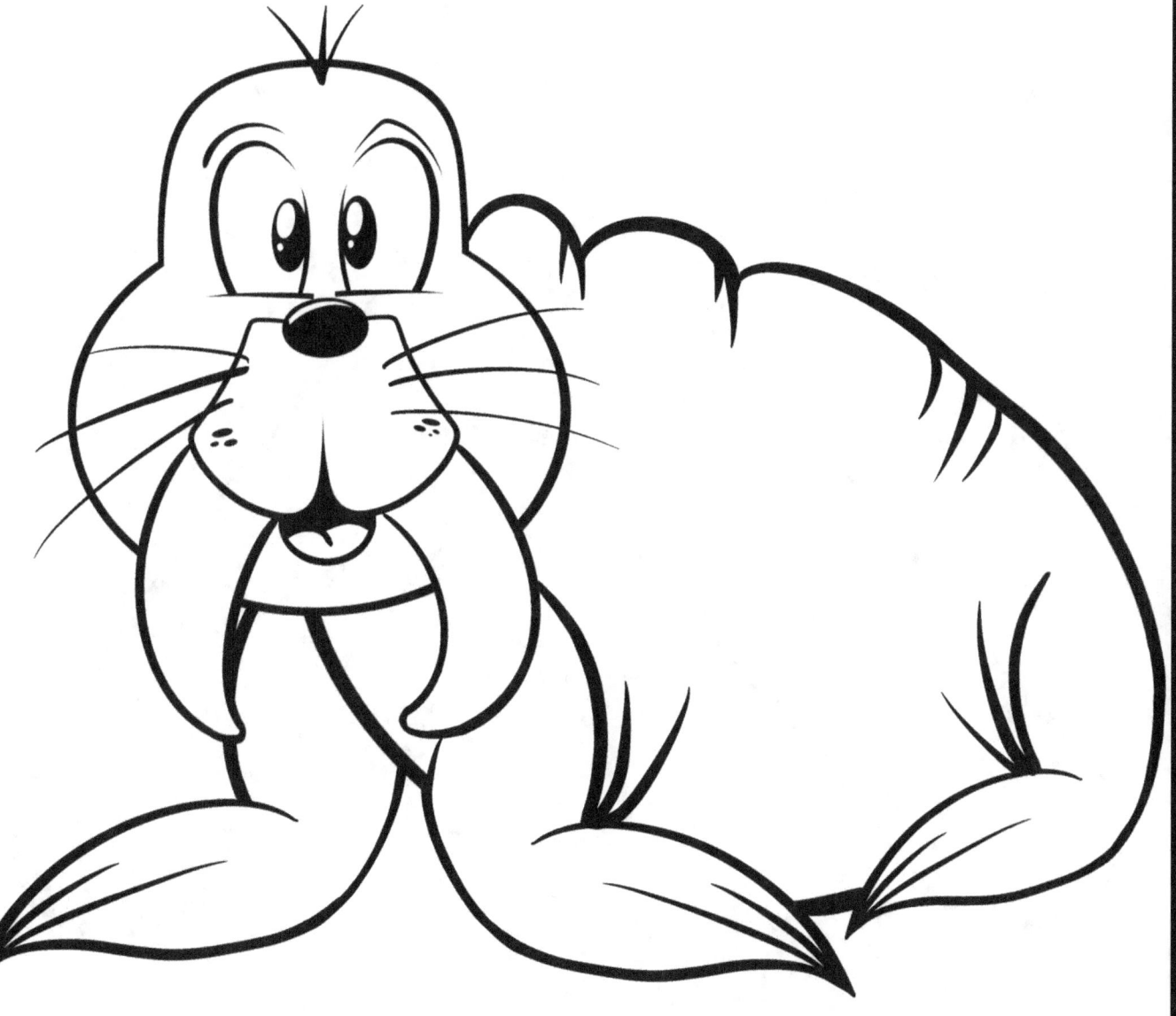

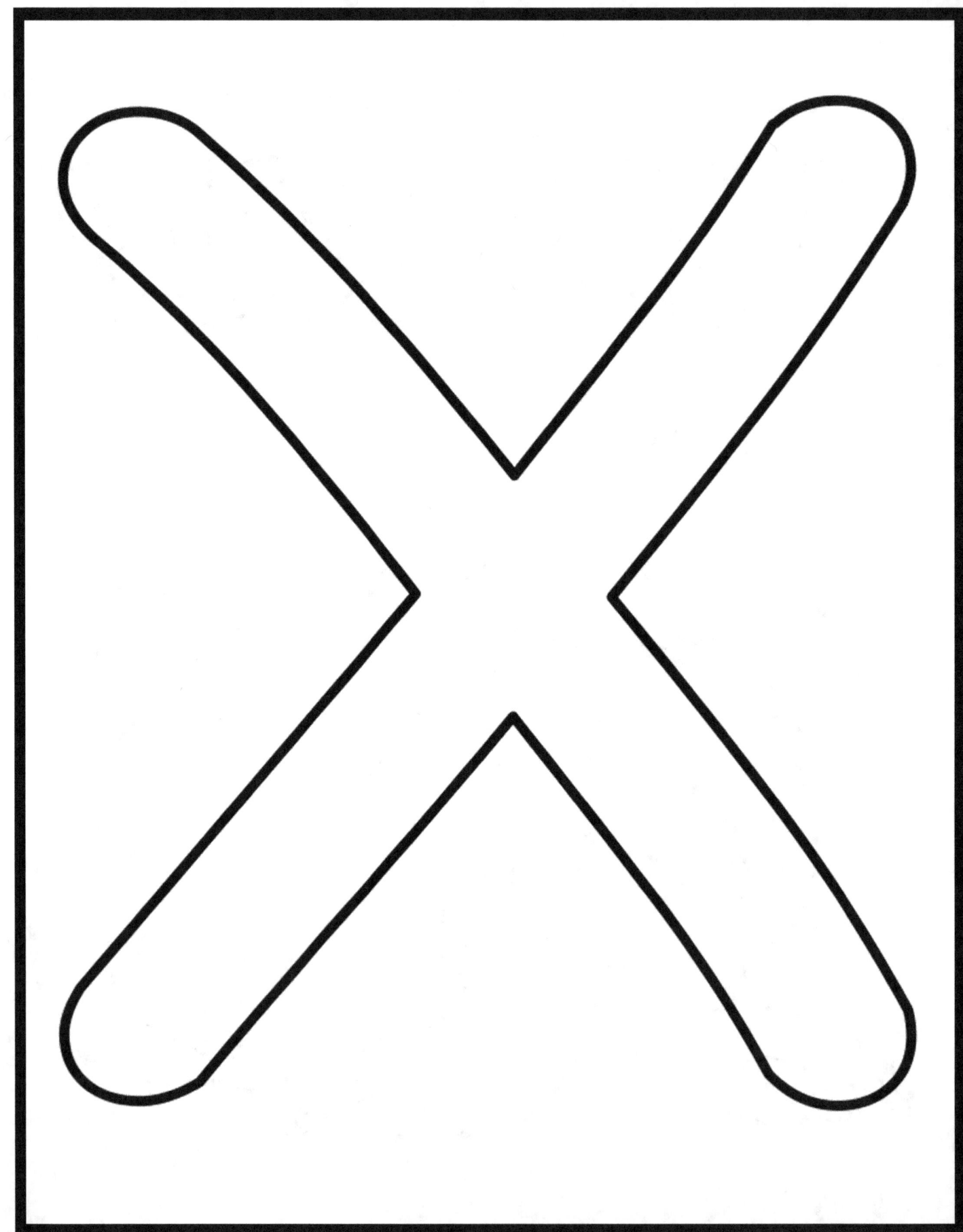

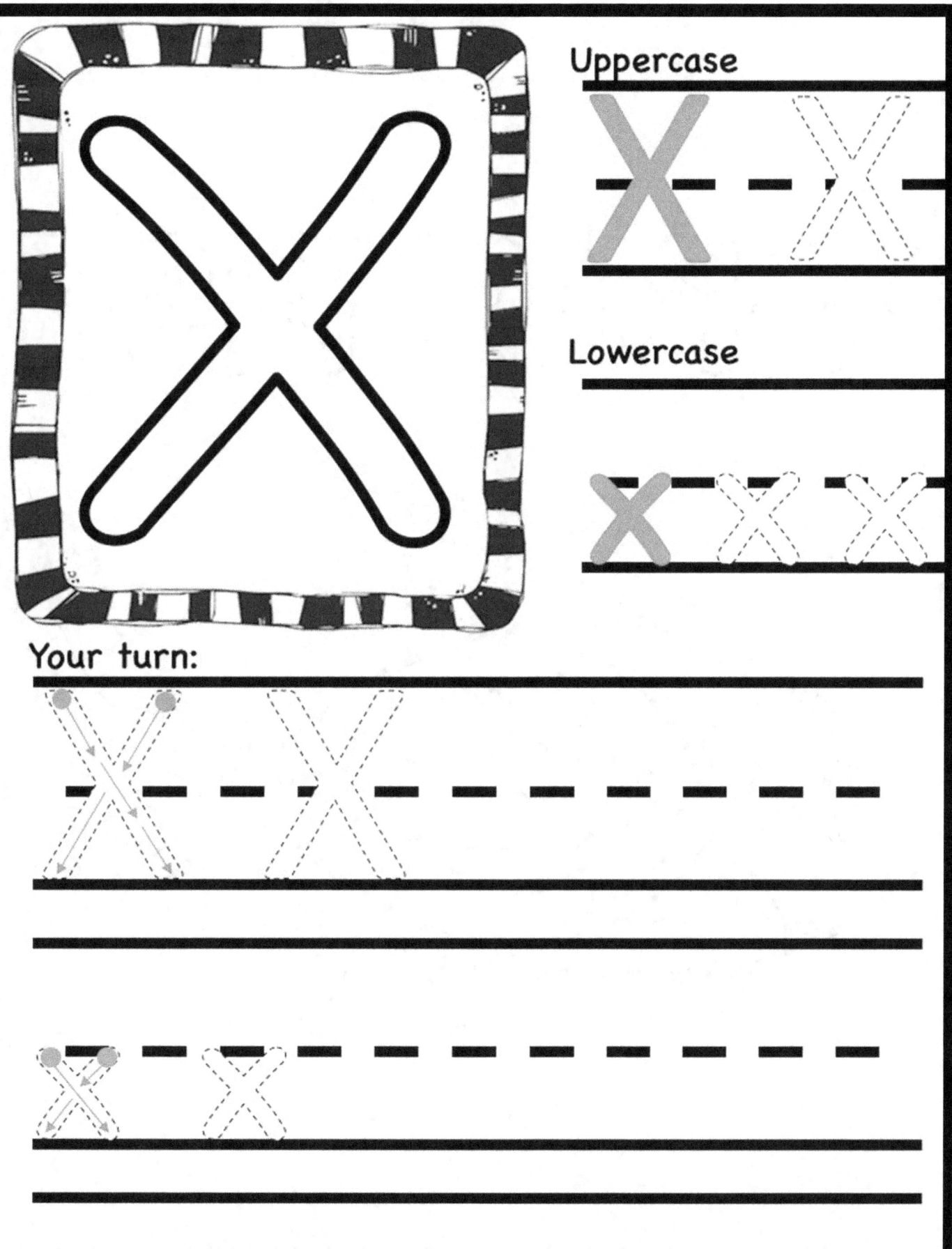

X-RAY FISH

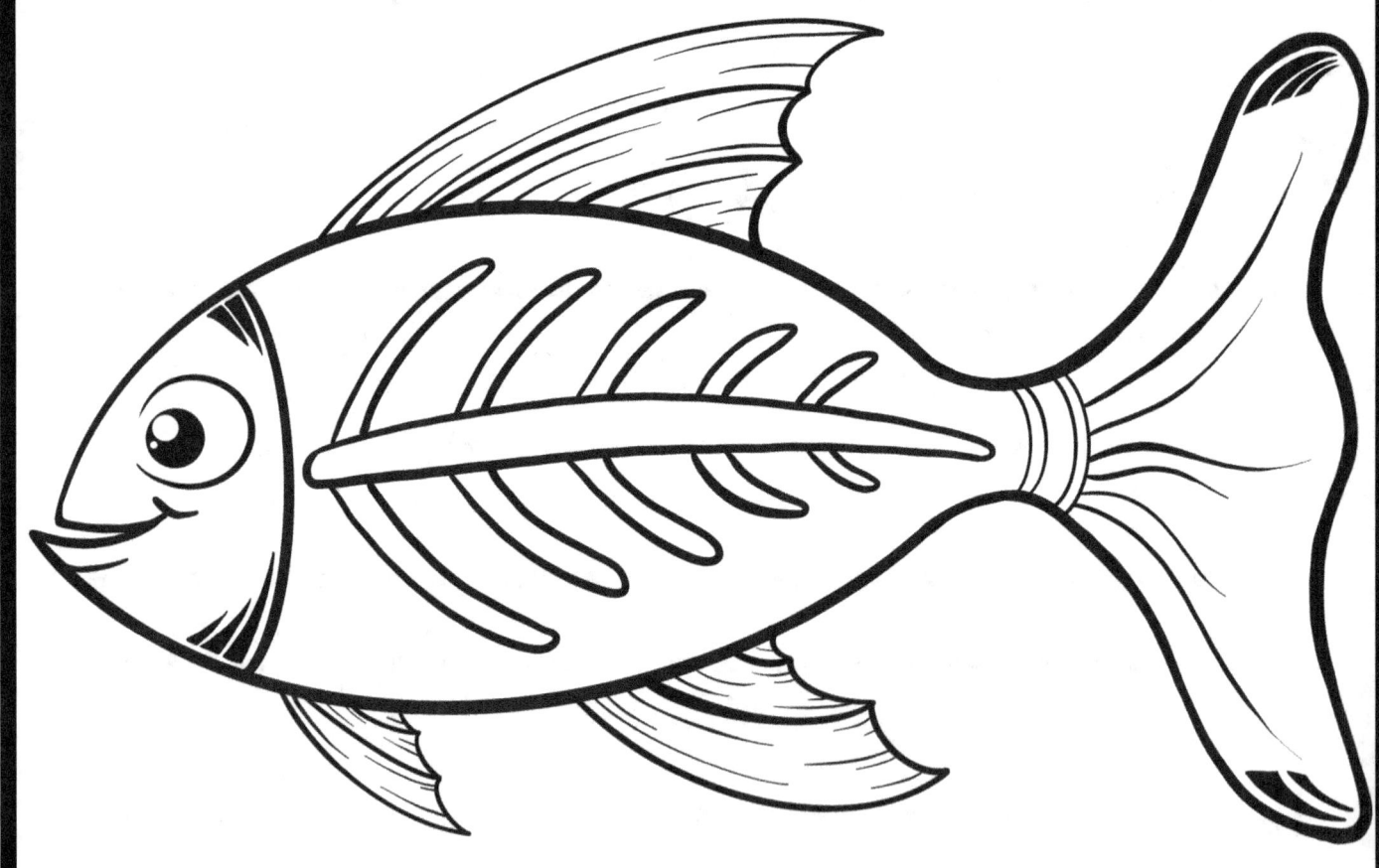

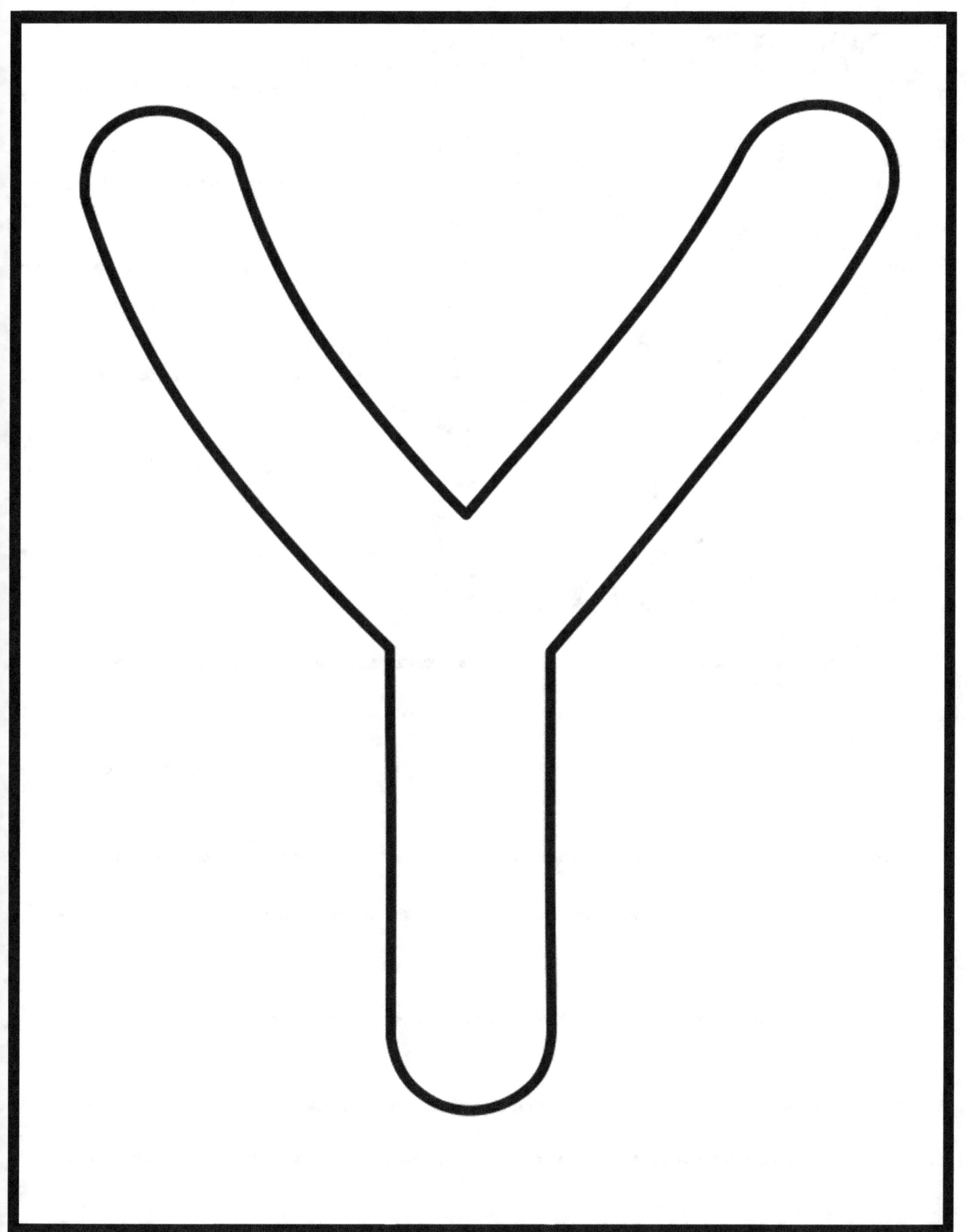

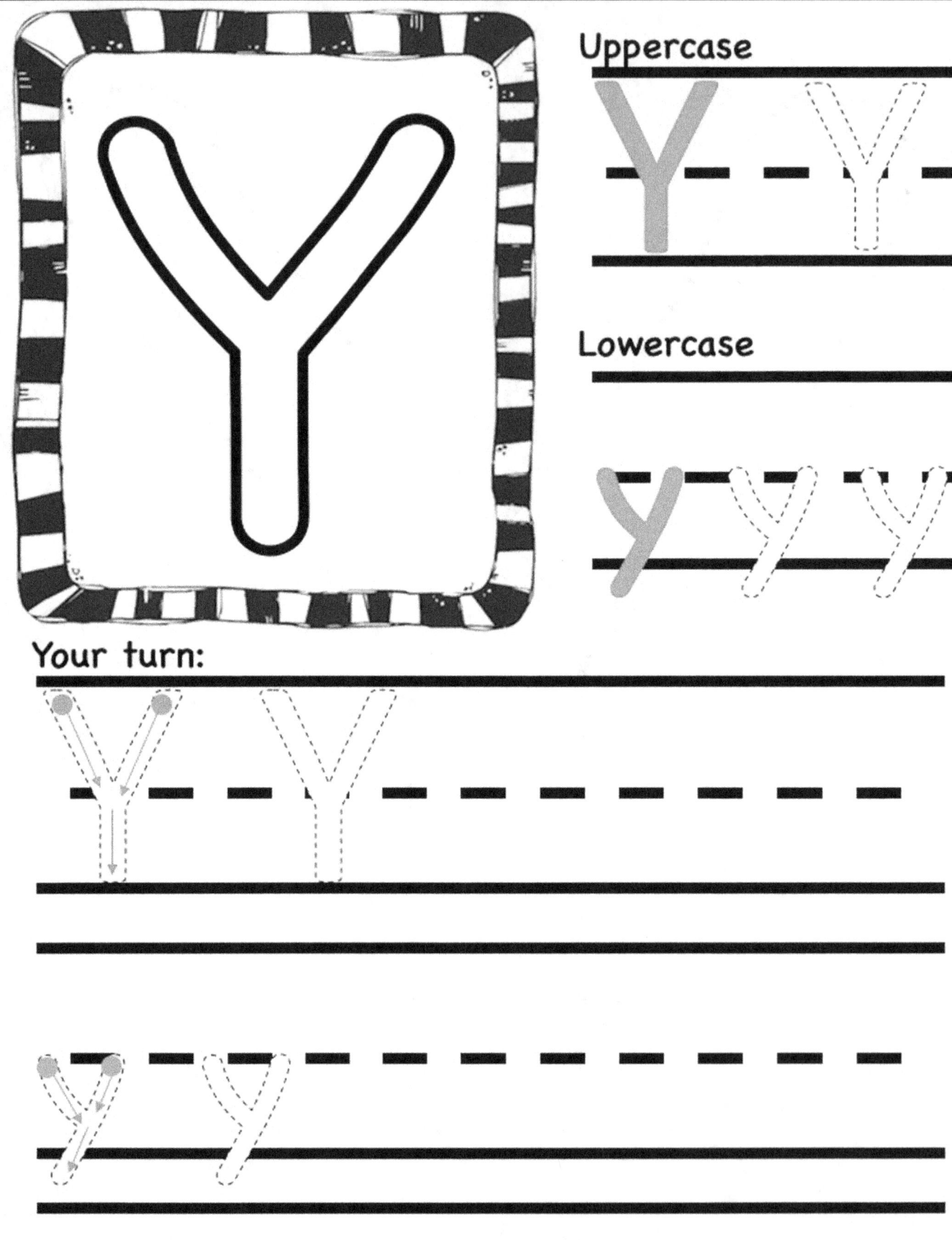

Uppercase

Lowercase

Your turn:

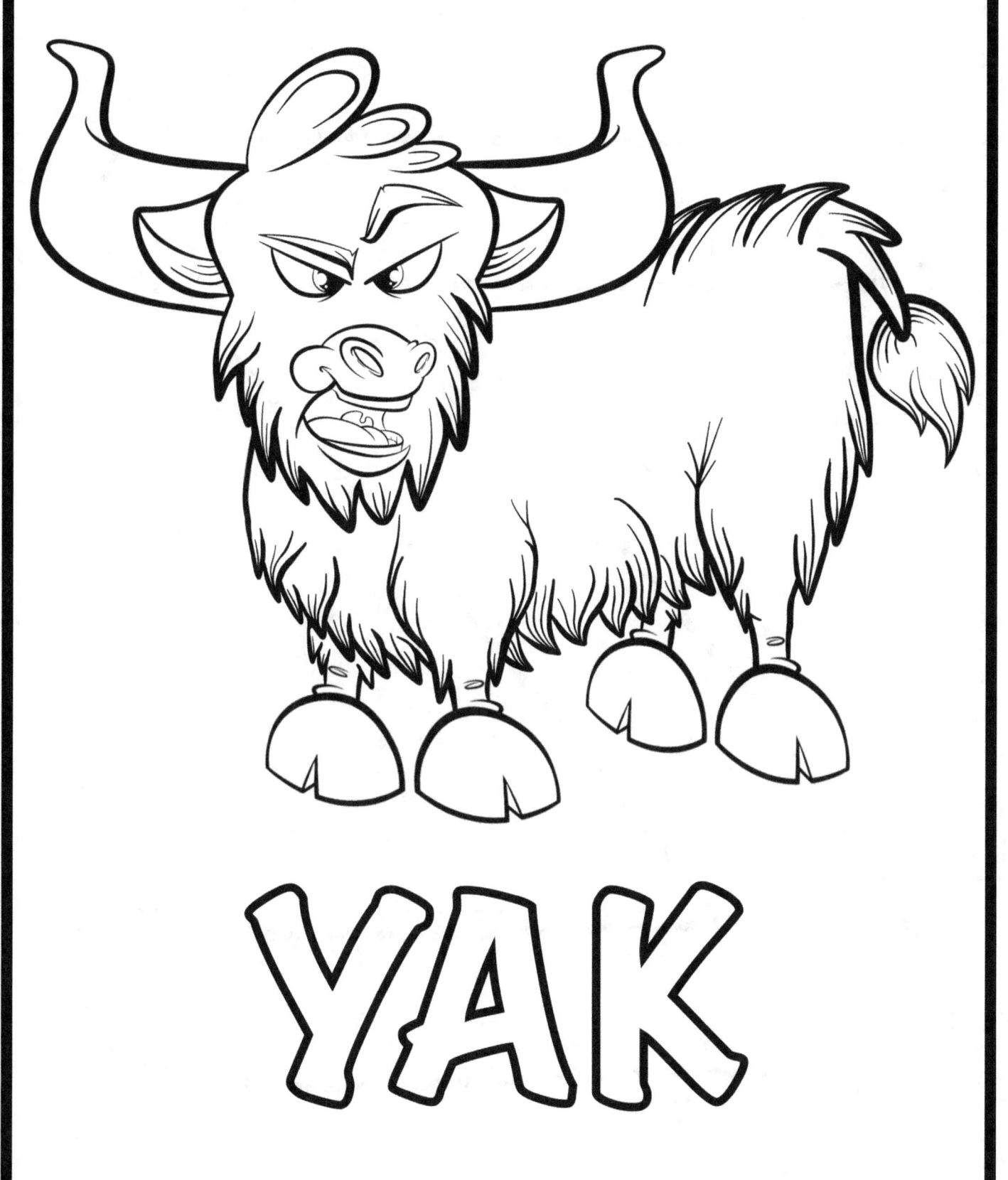

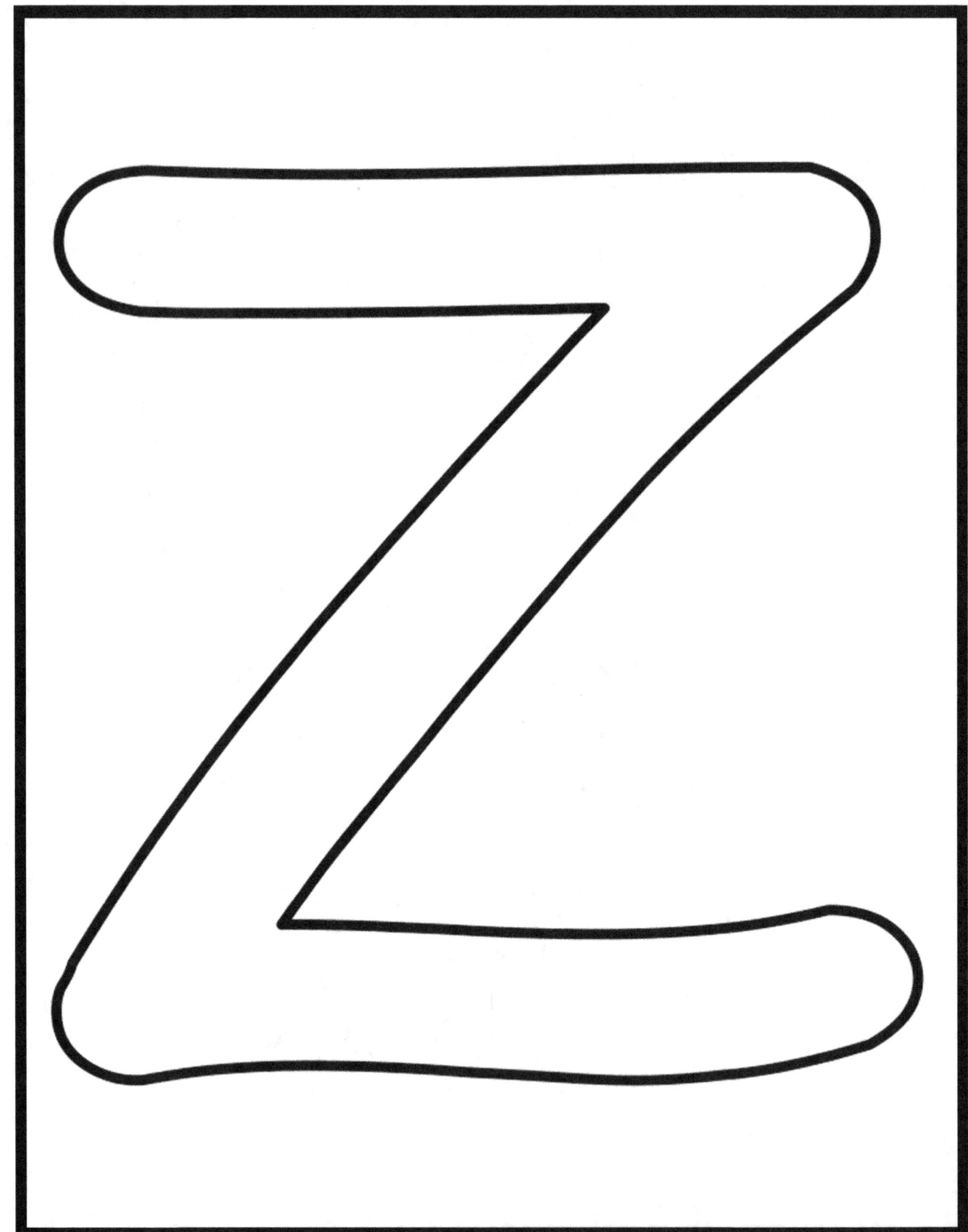

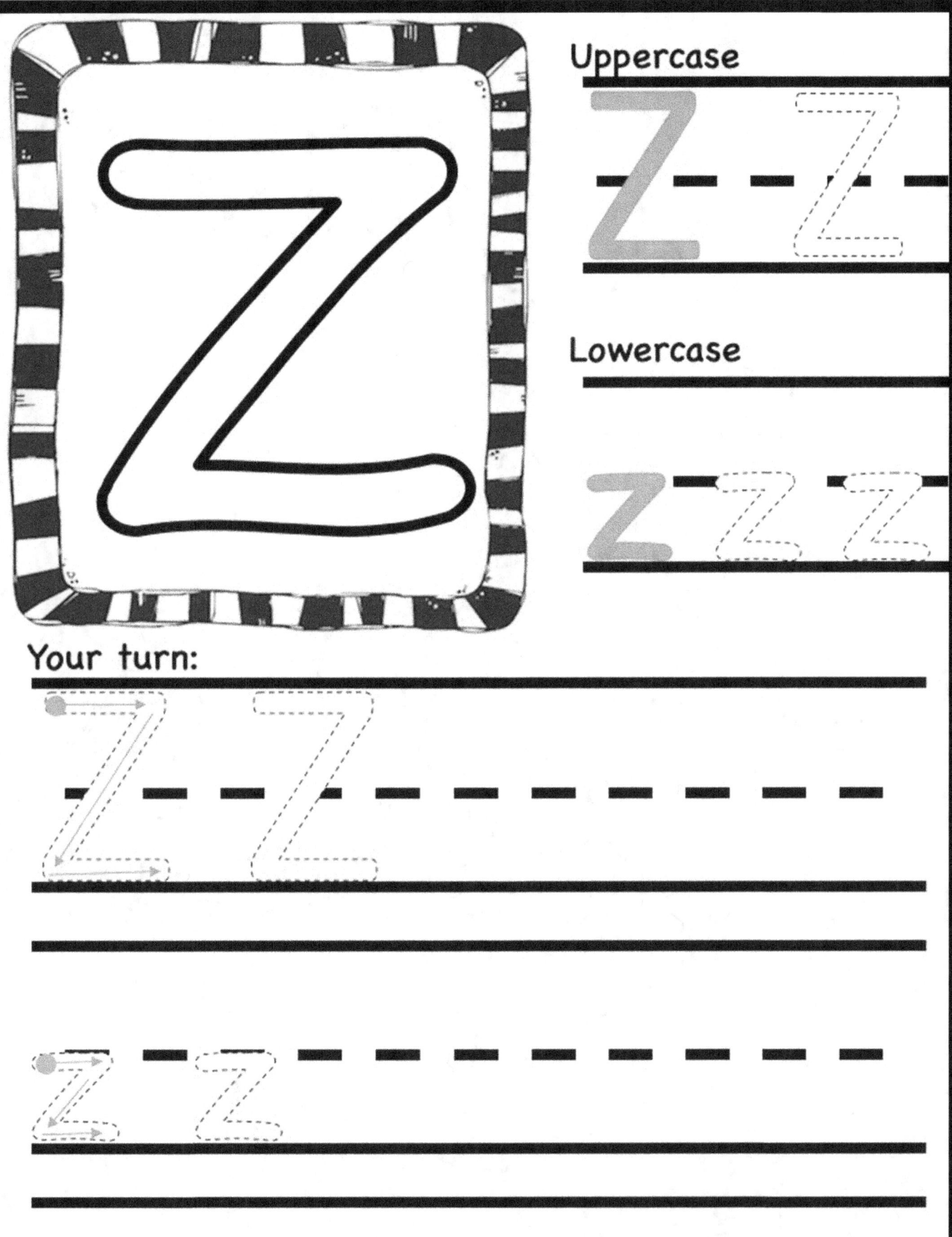

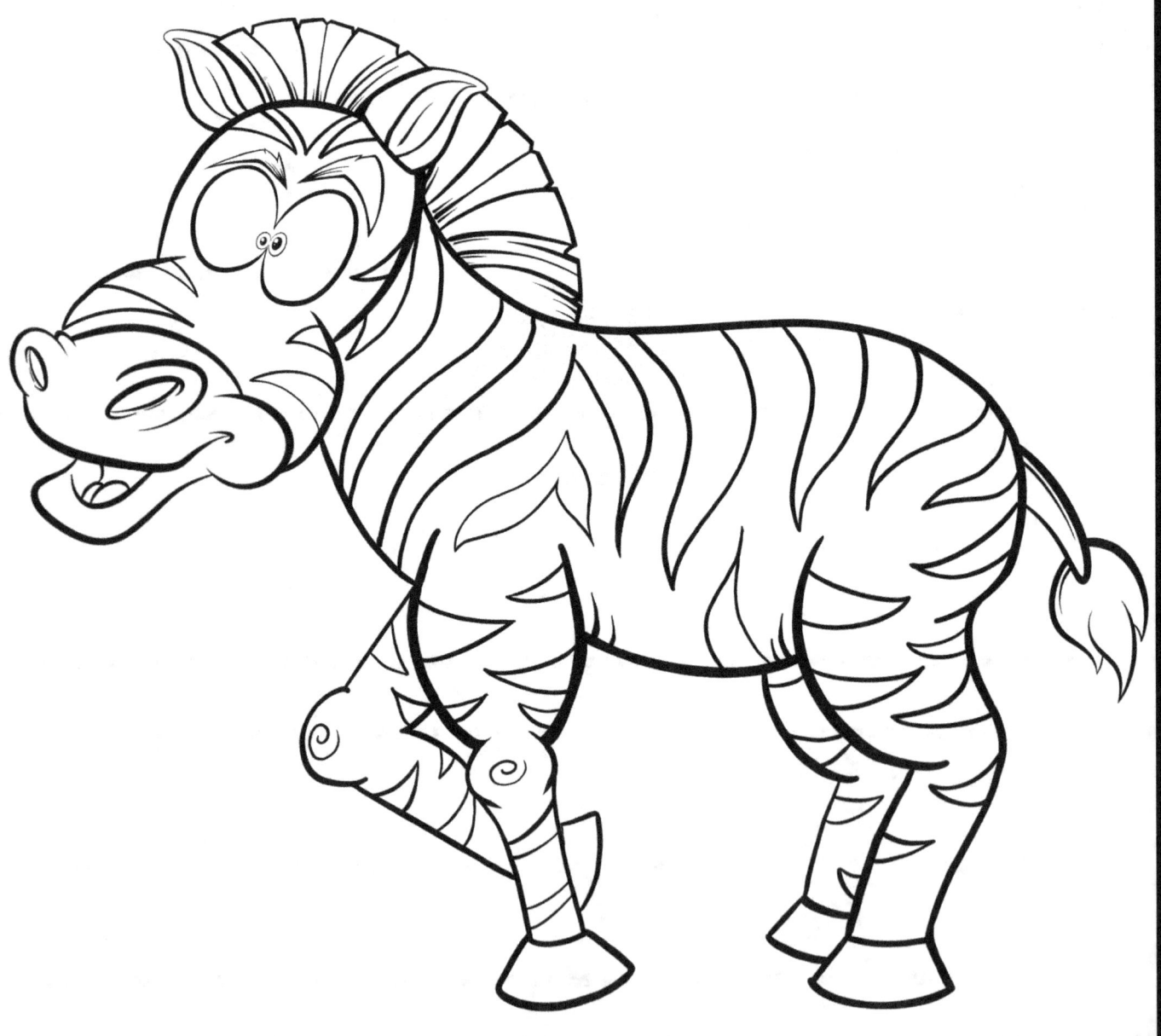

NUMBERS

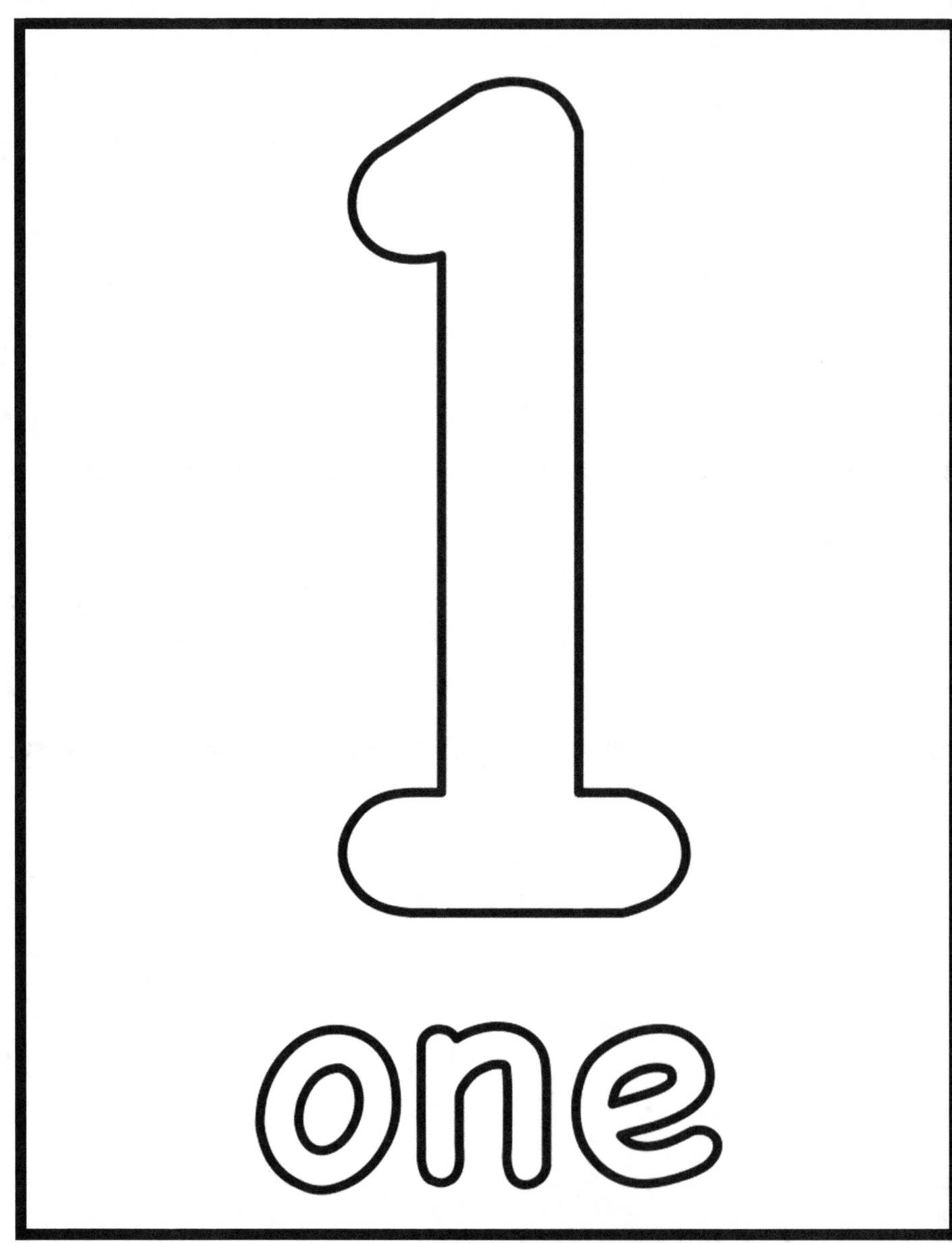

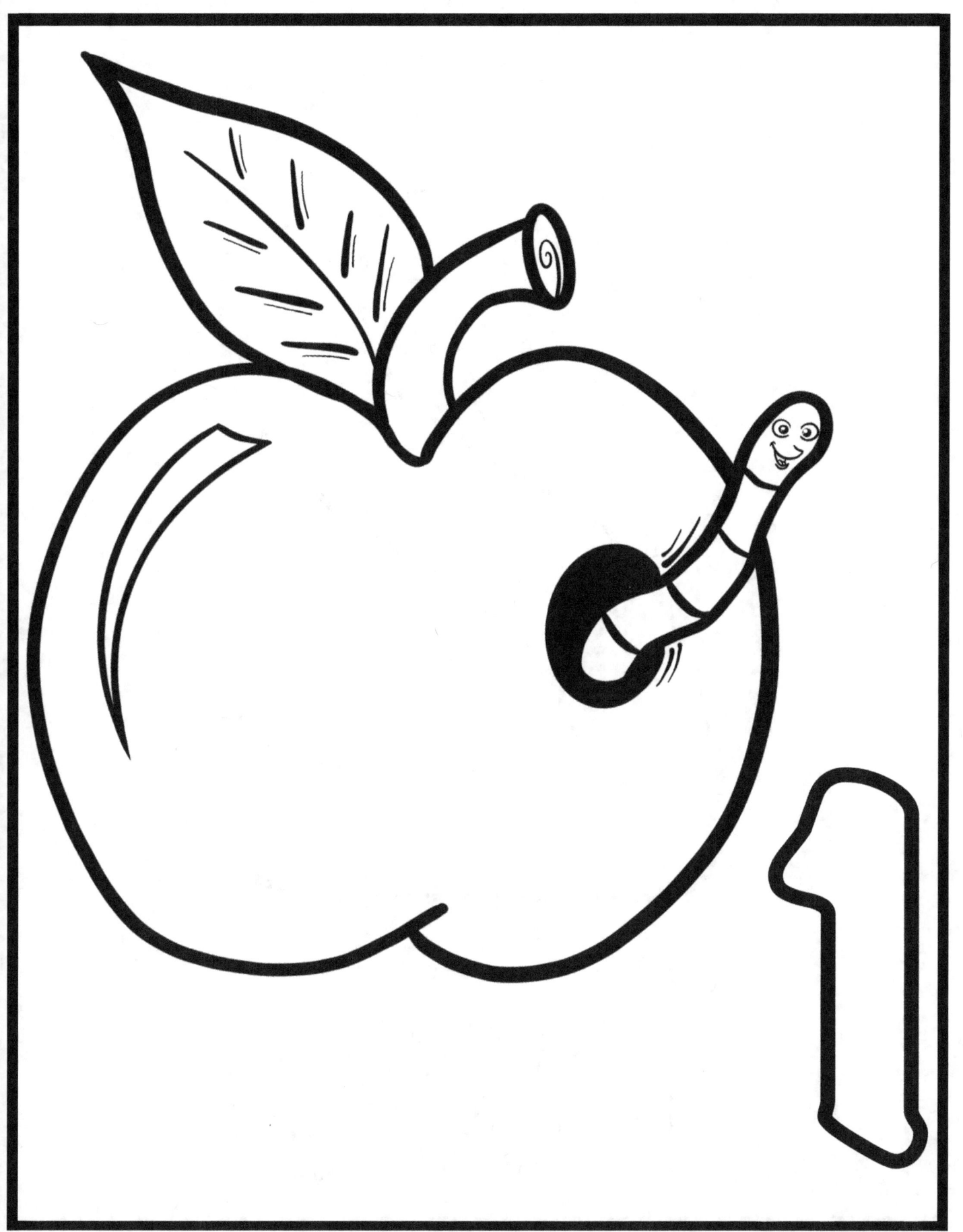

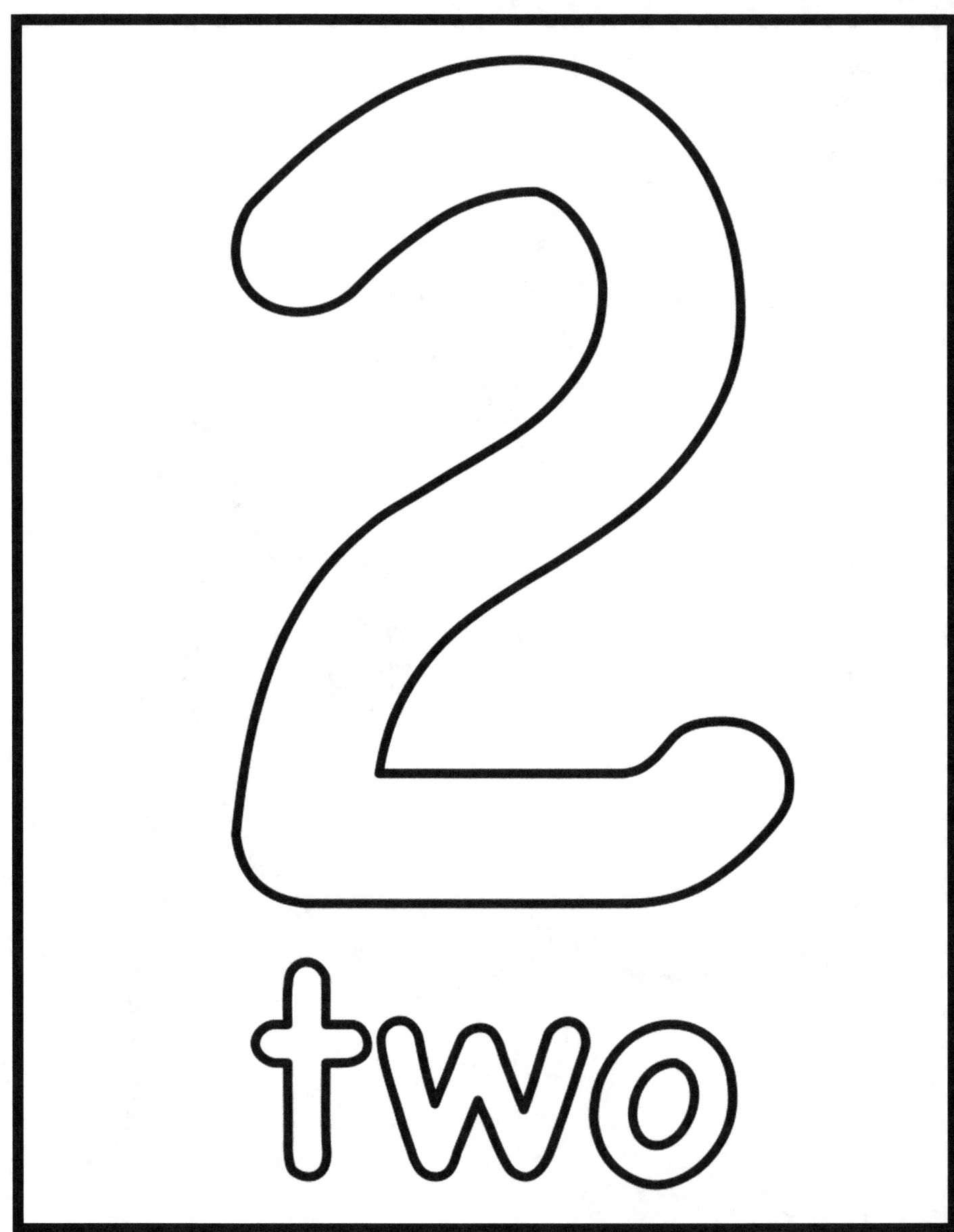

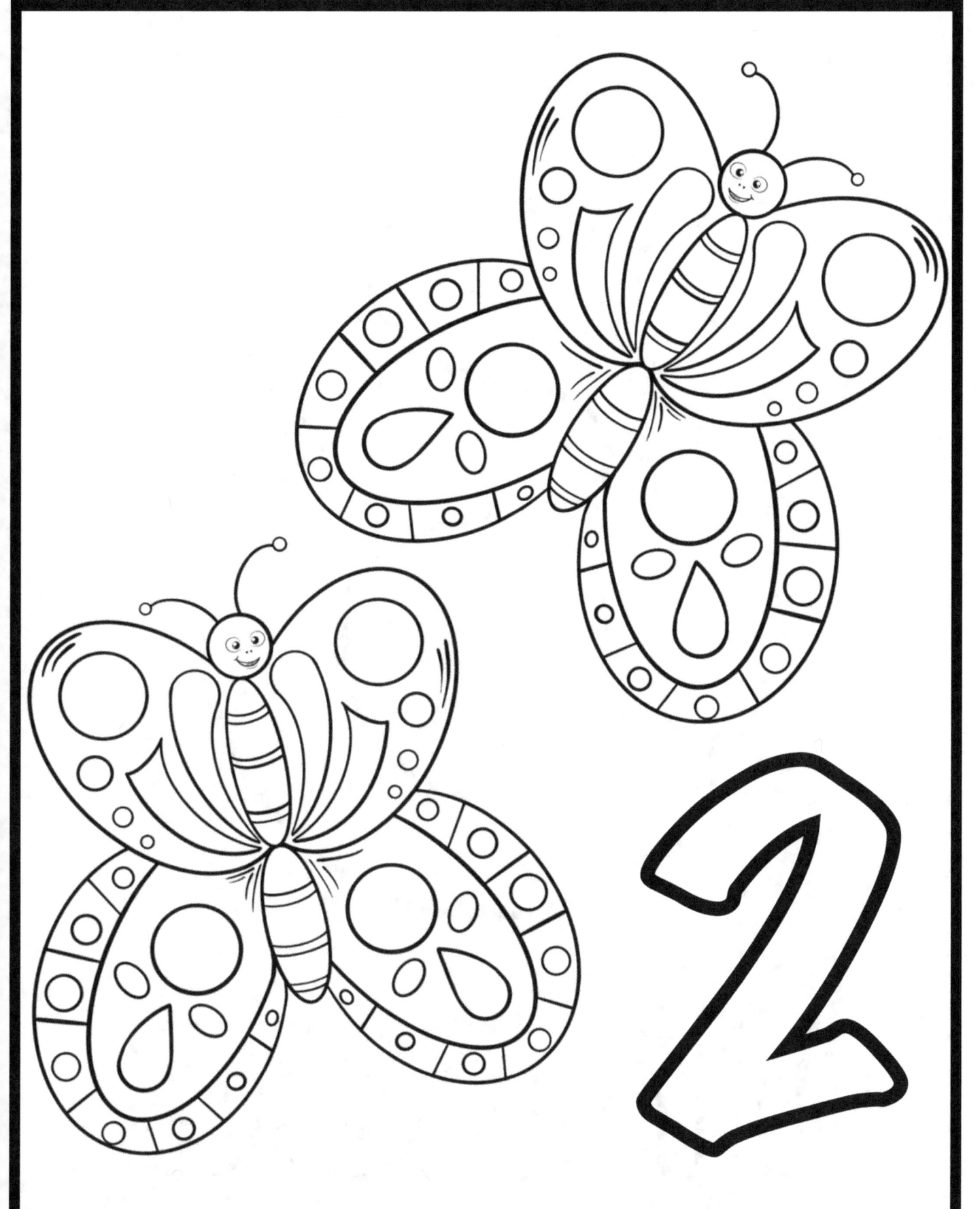

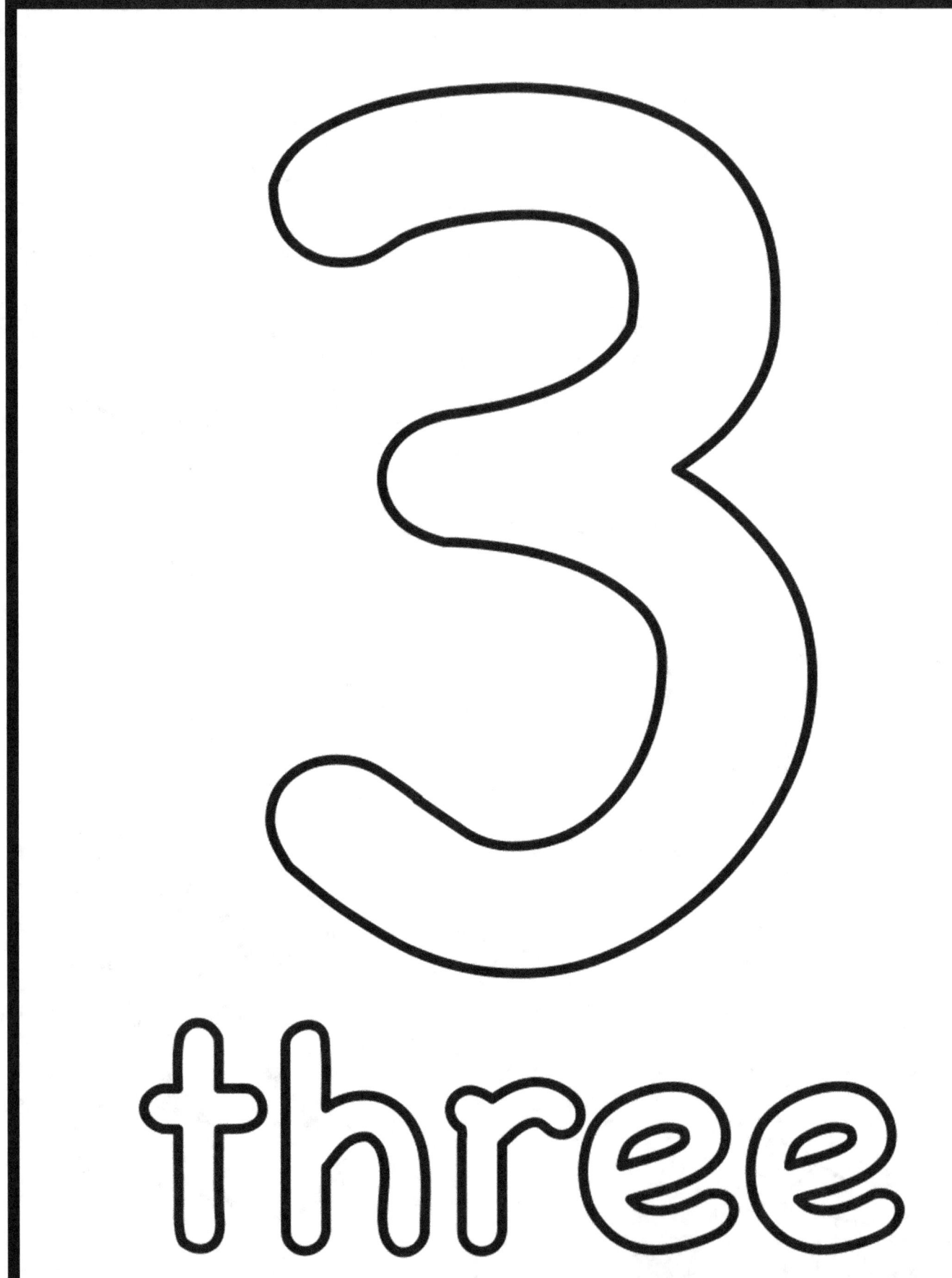

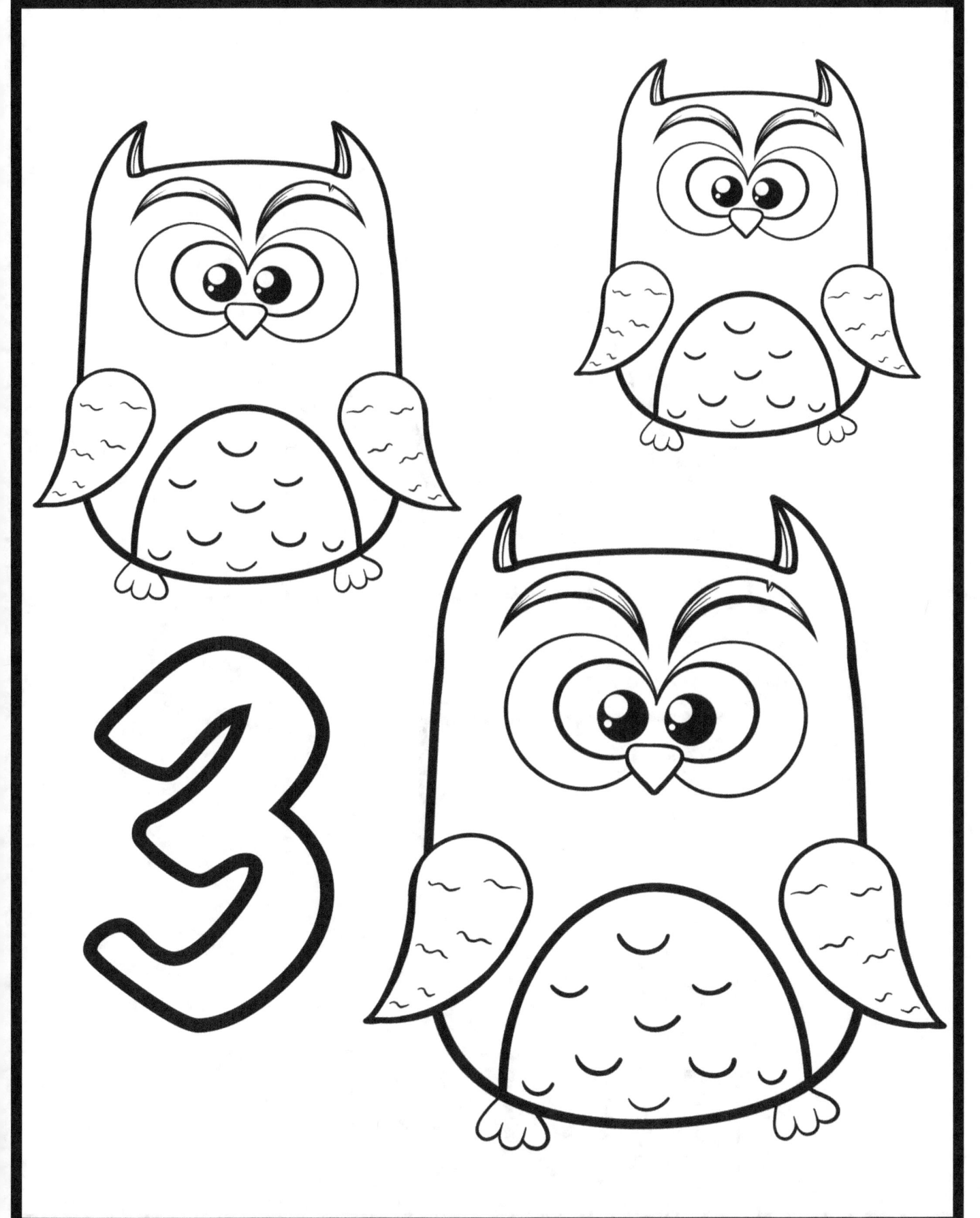

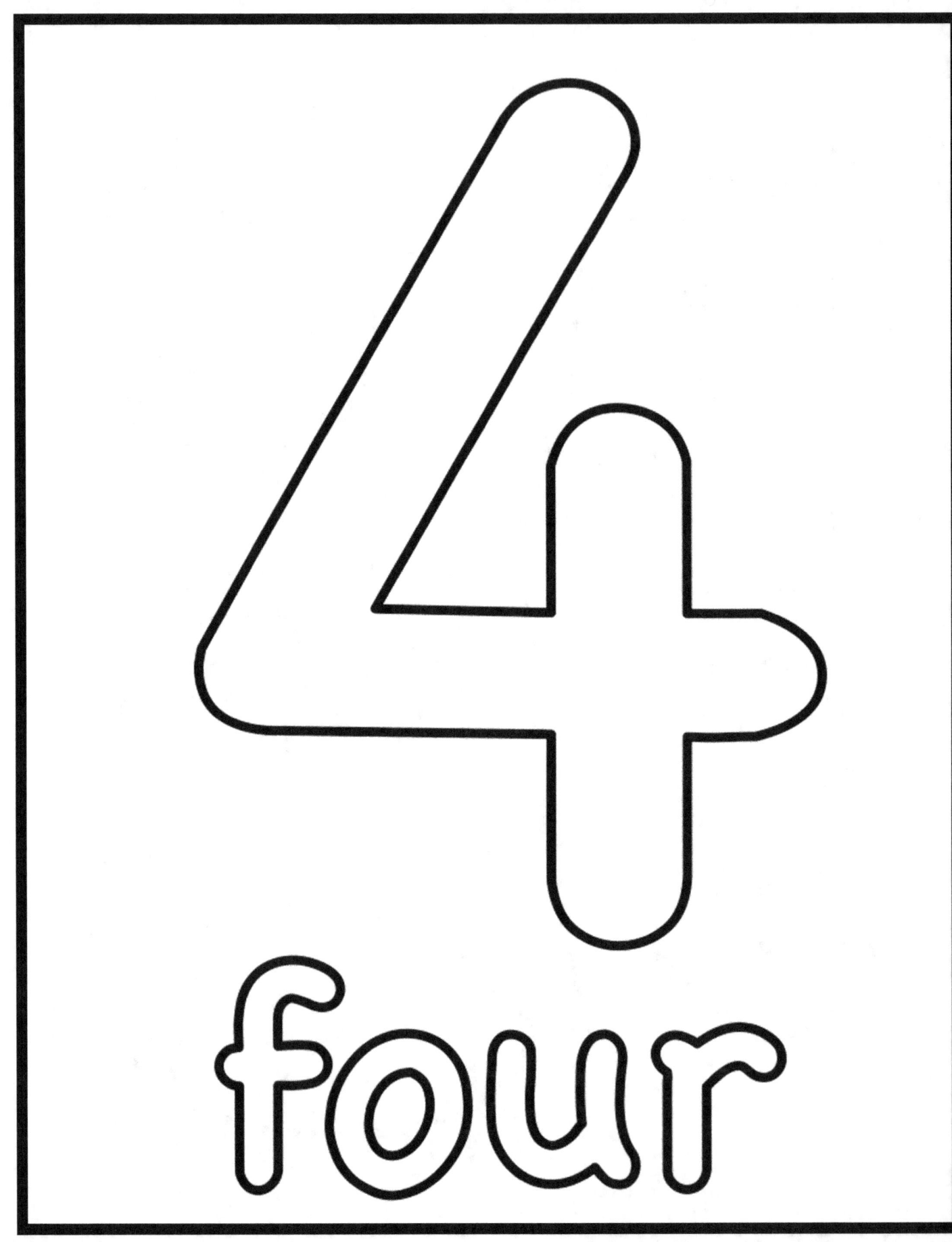

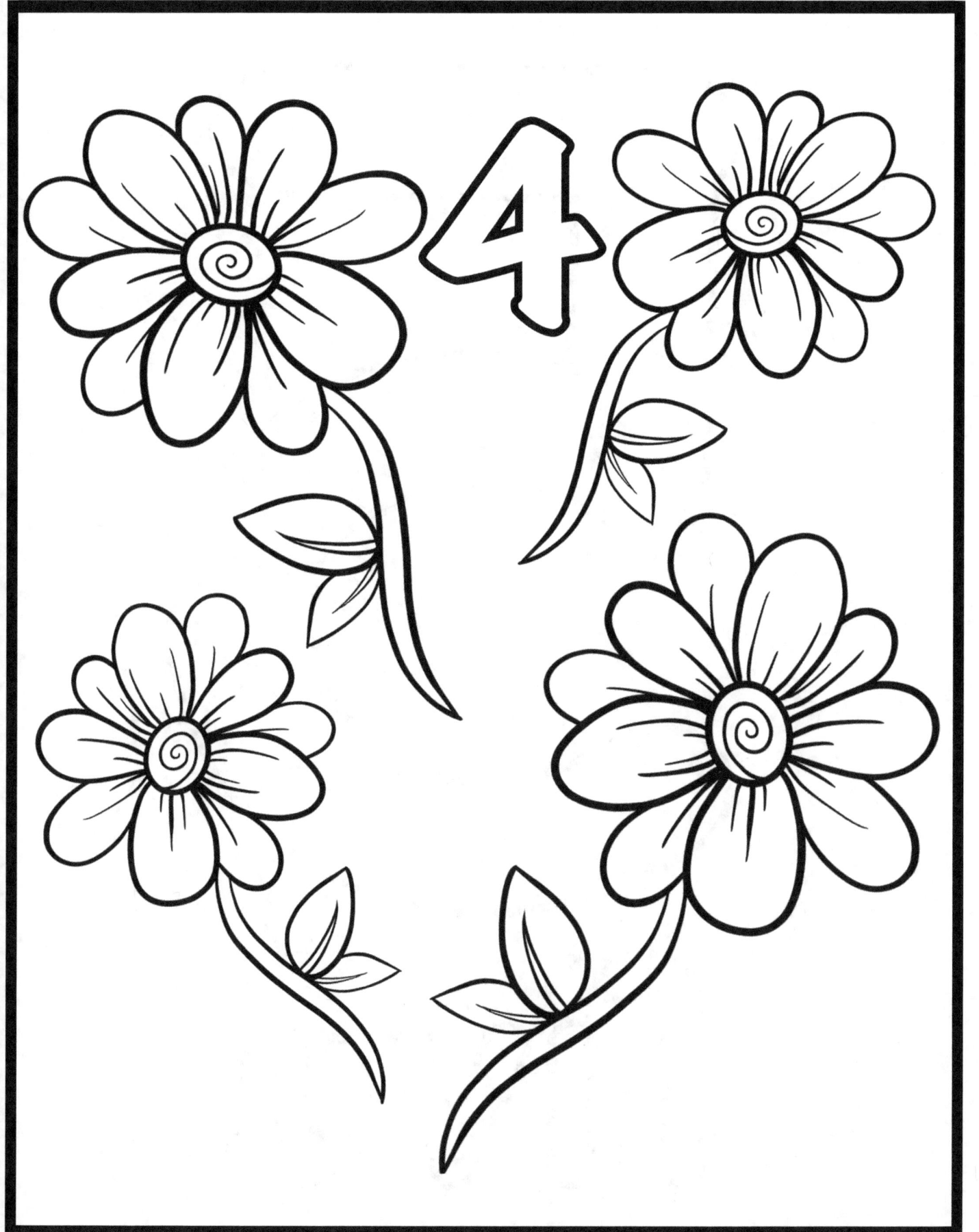

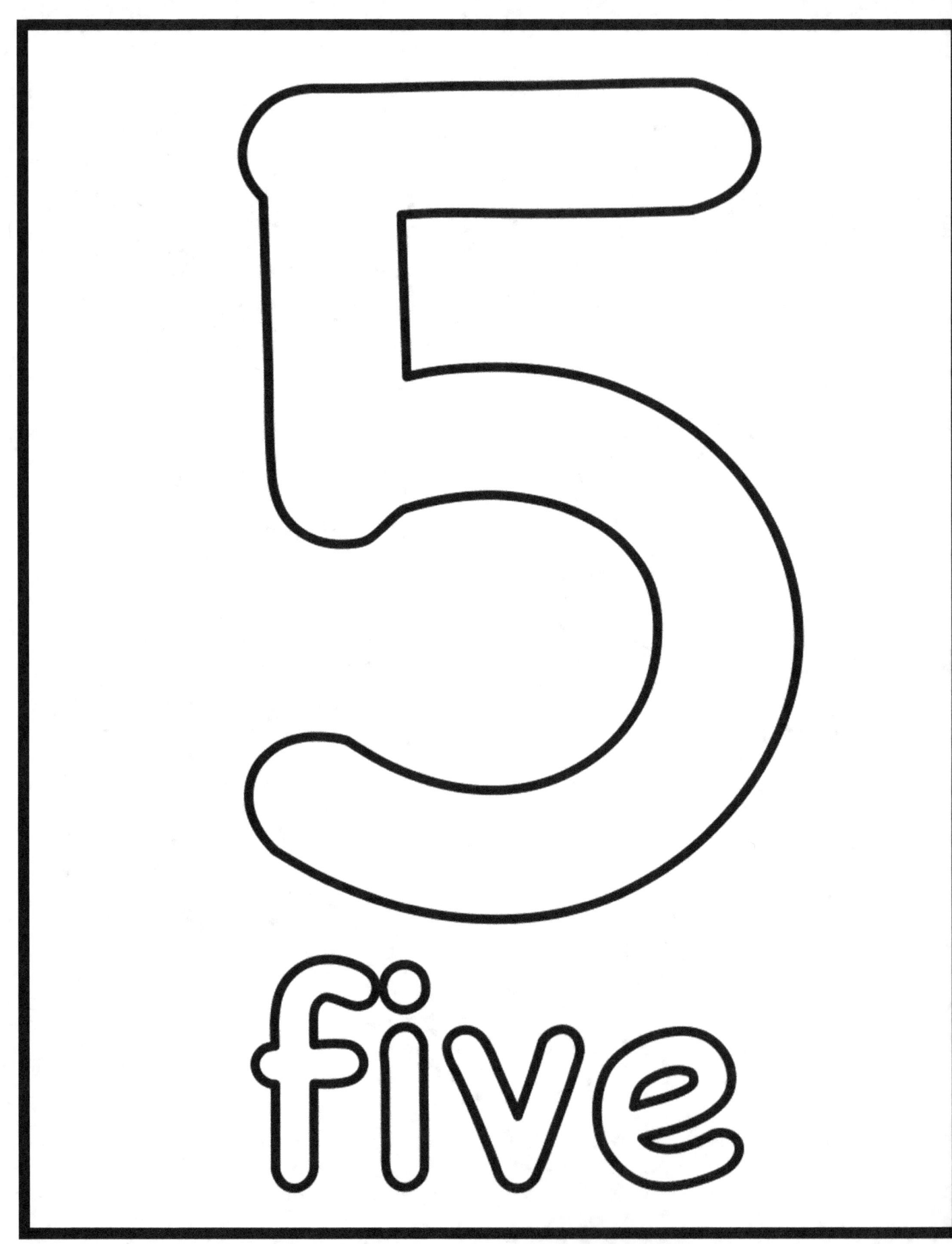

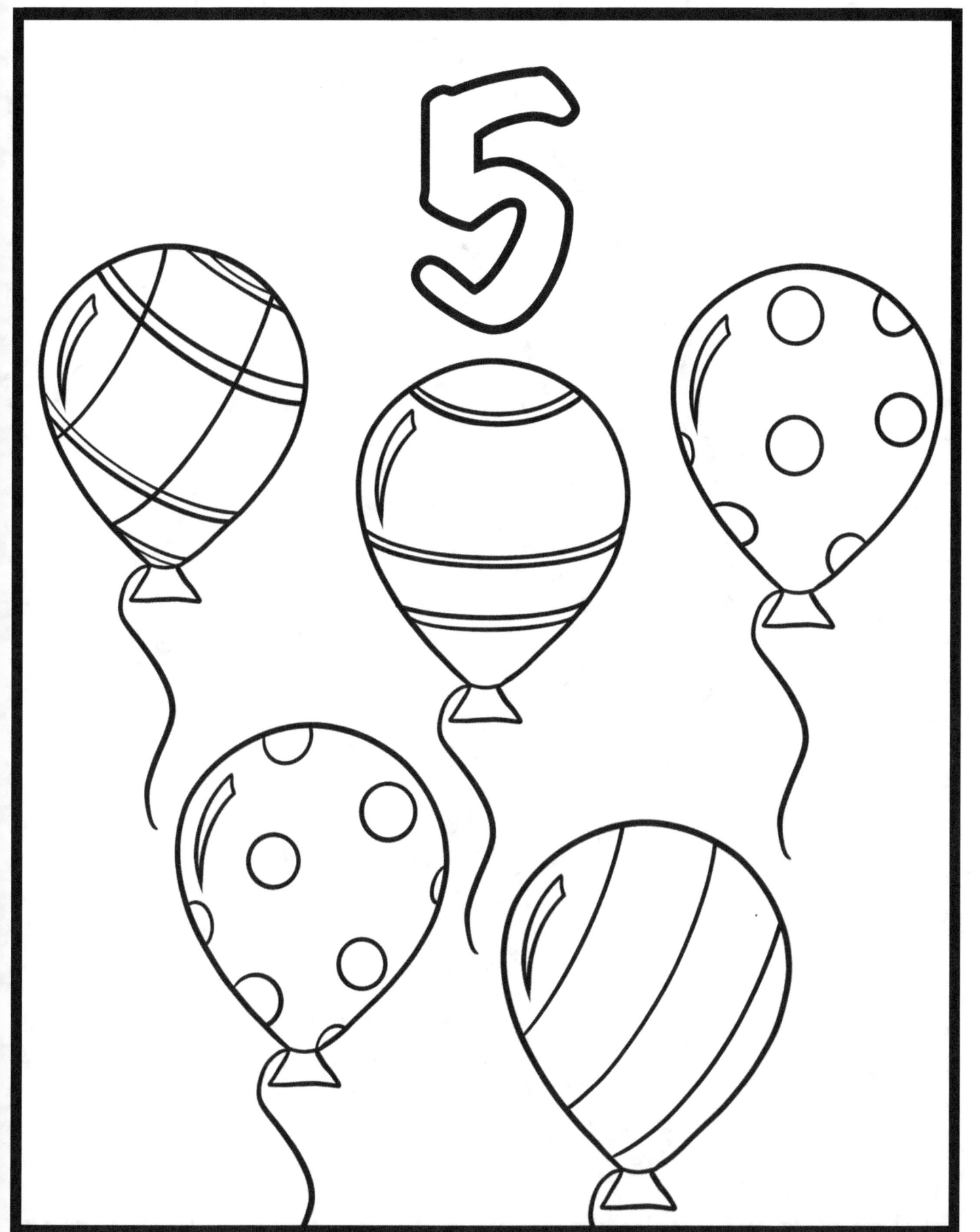

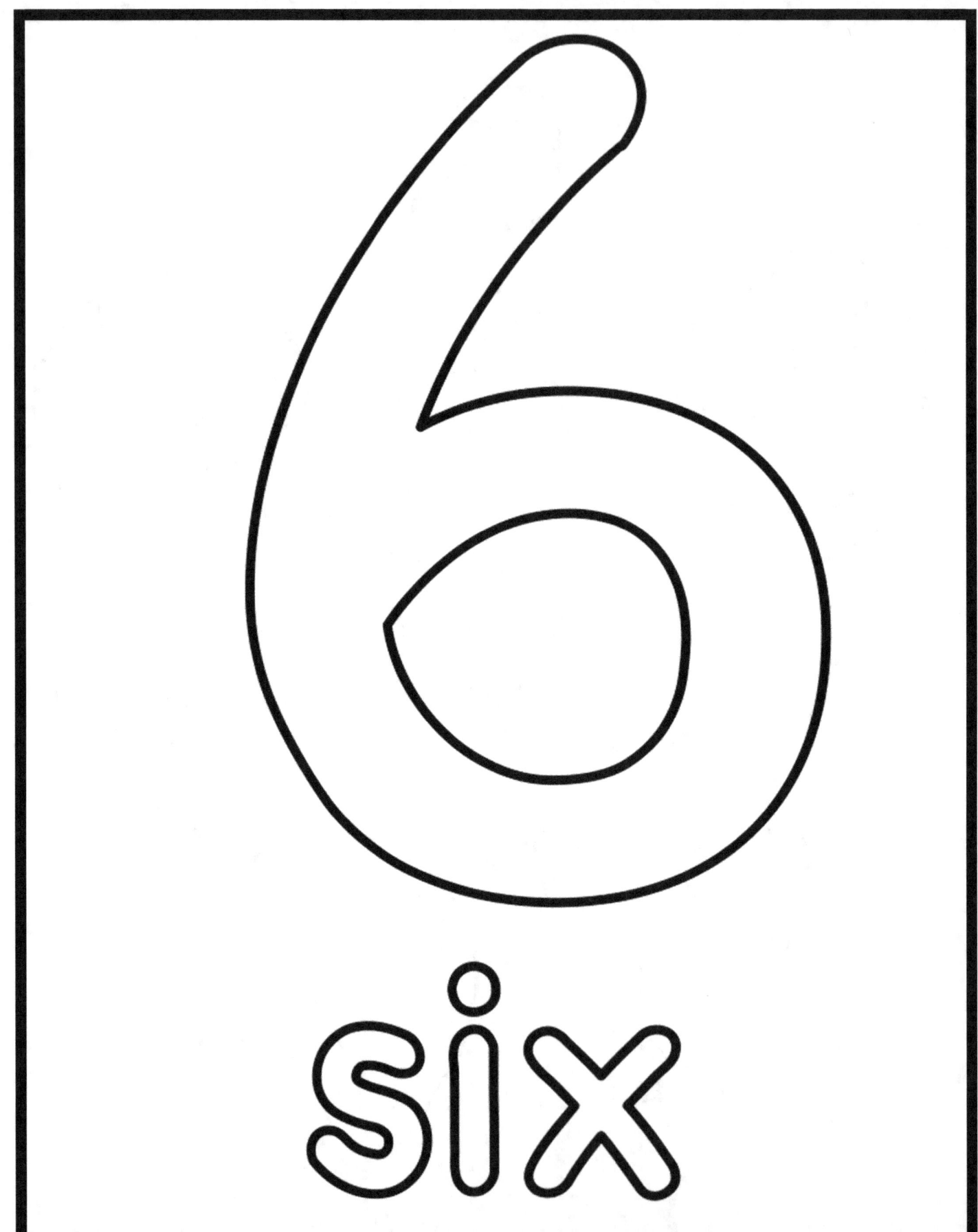

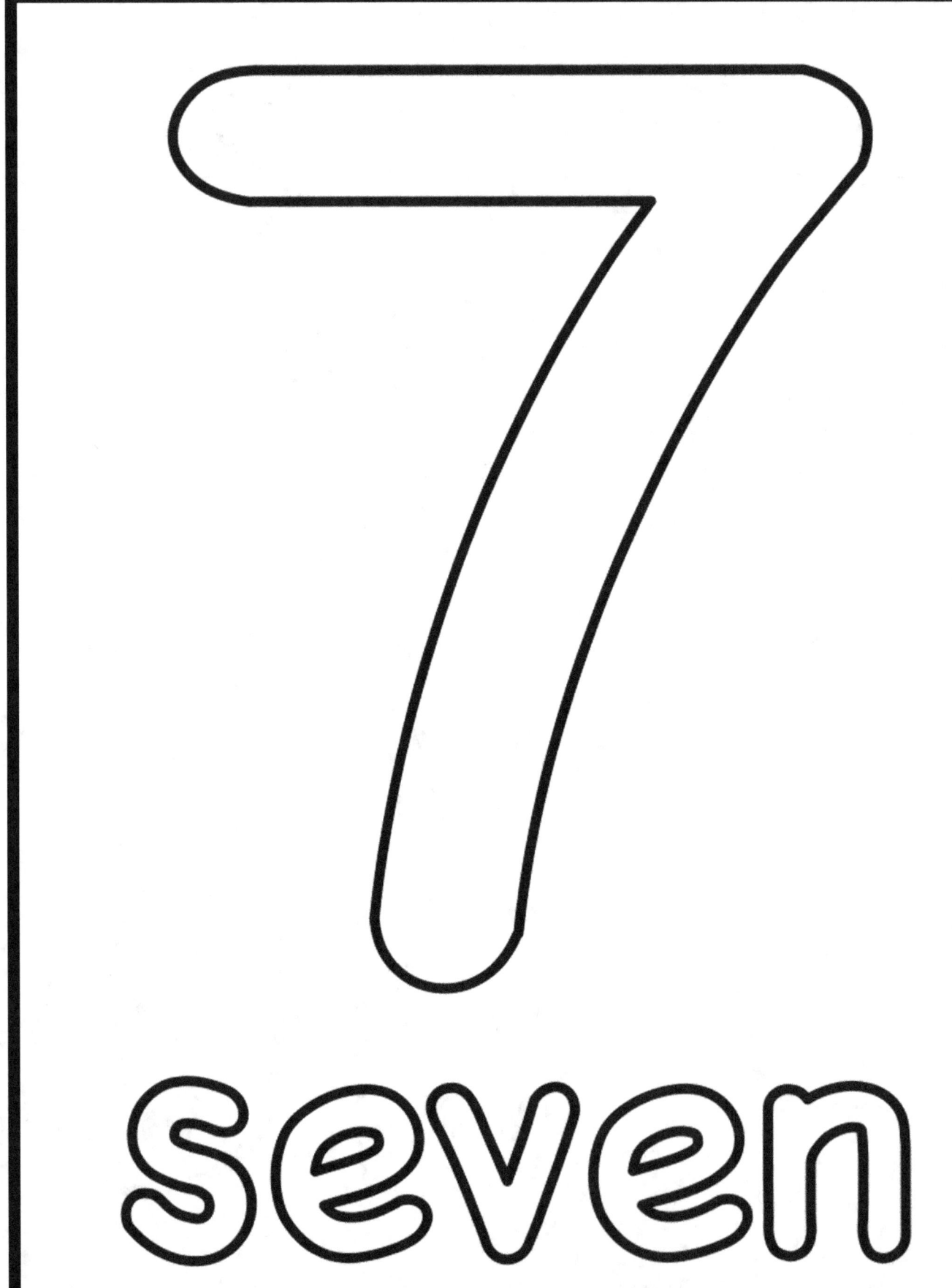

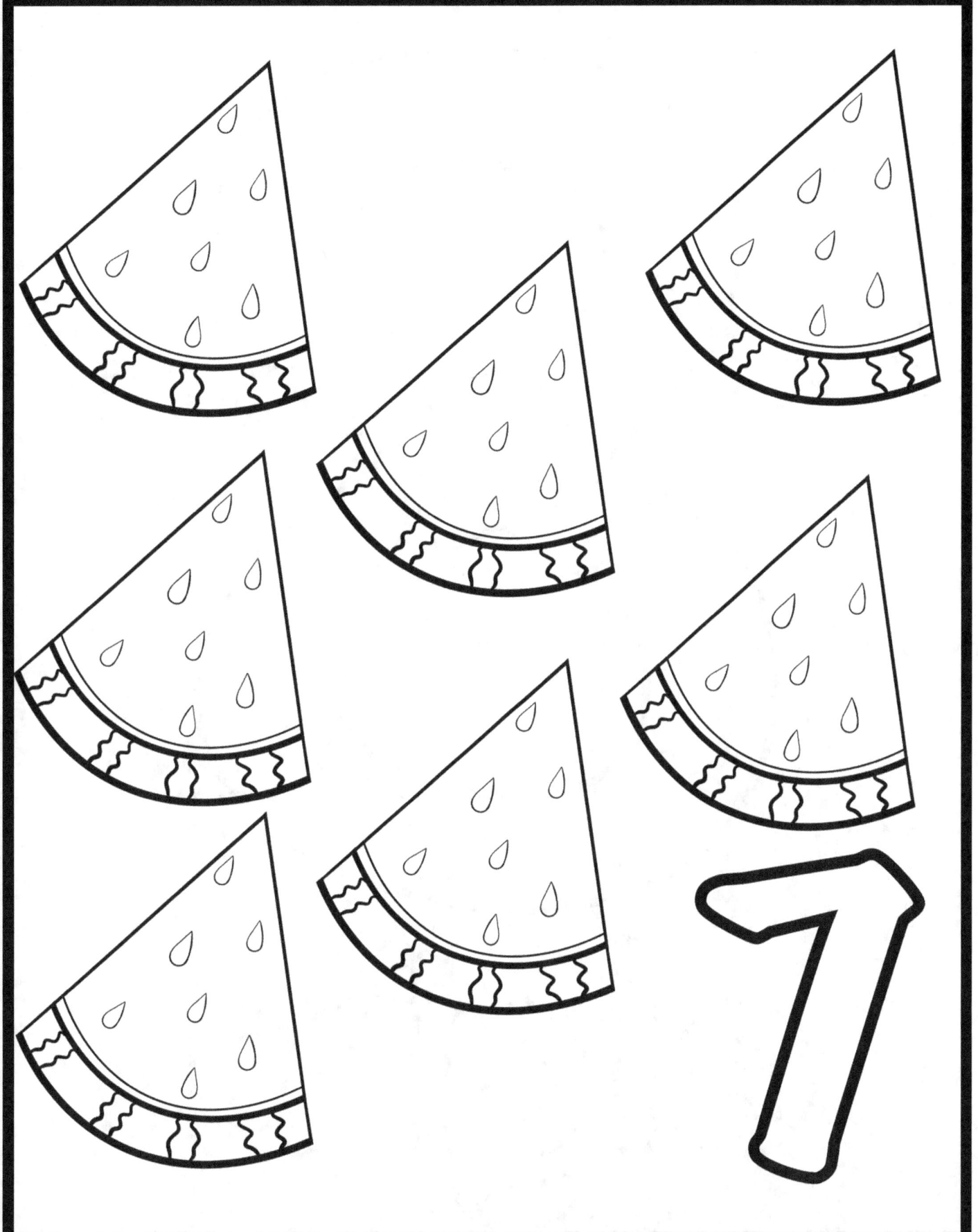

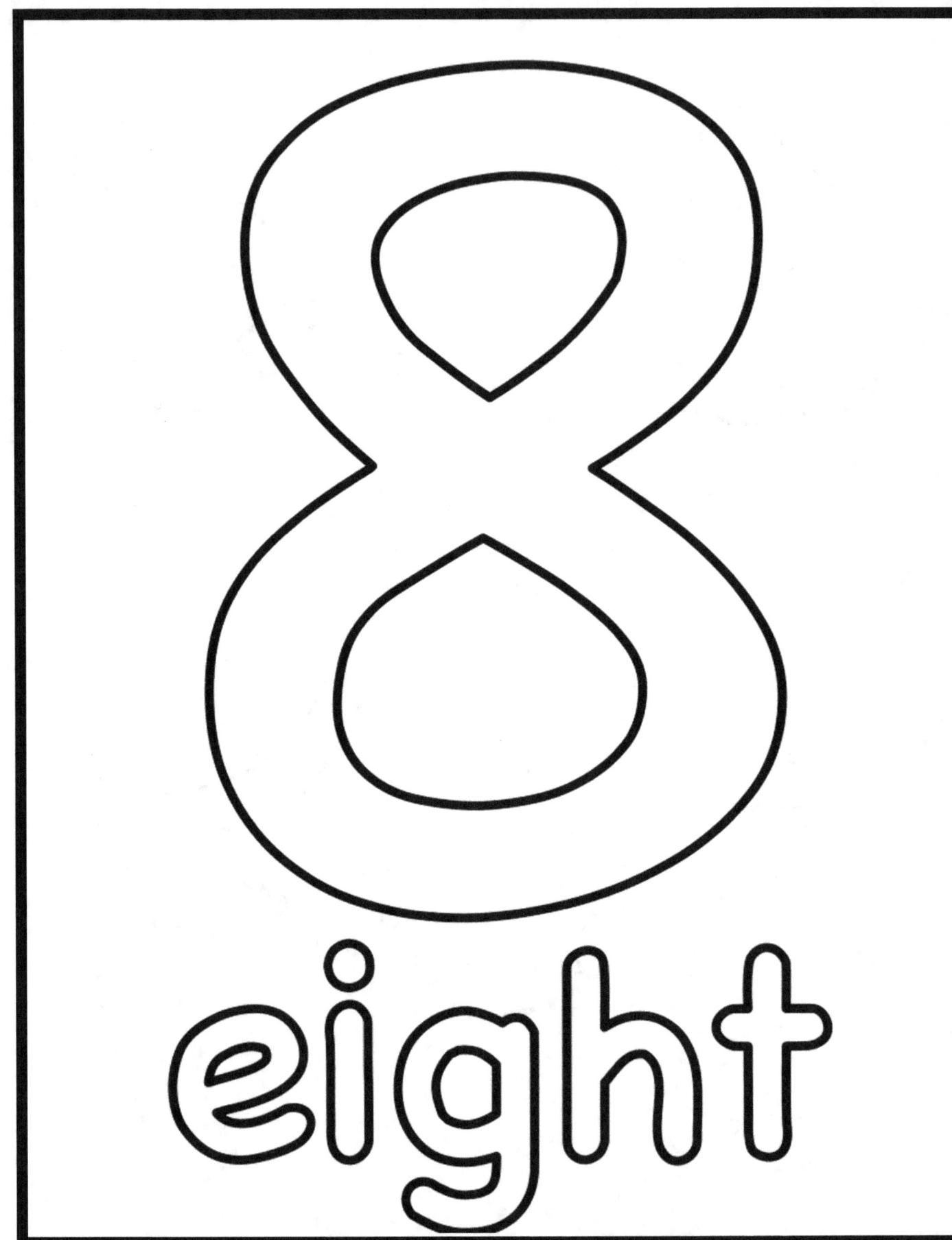

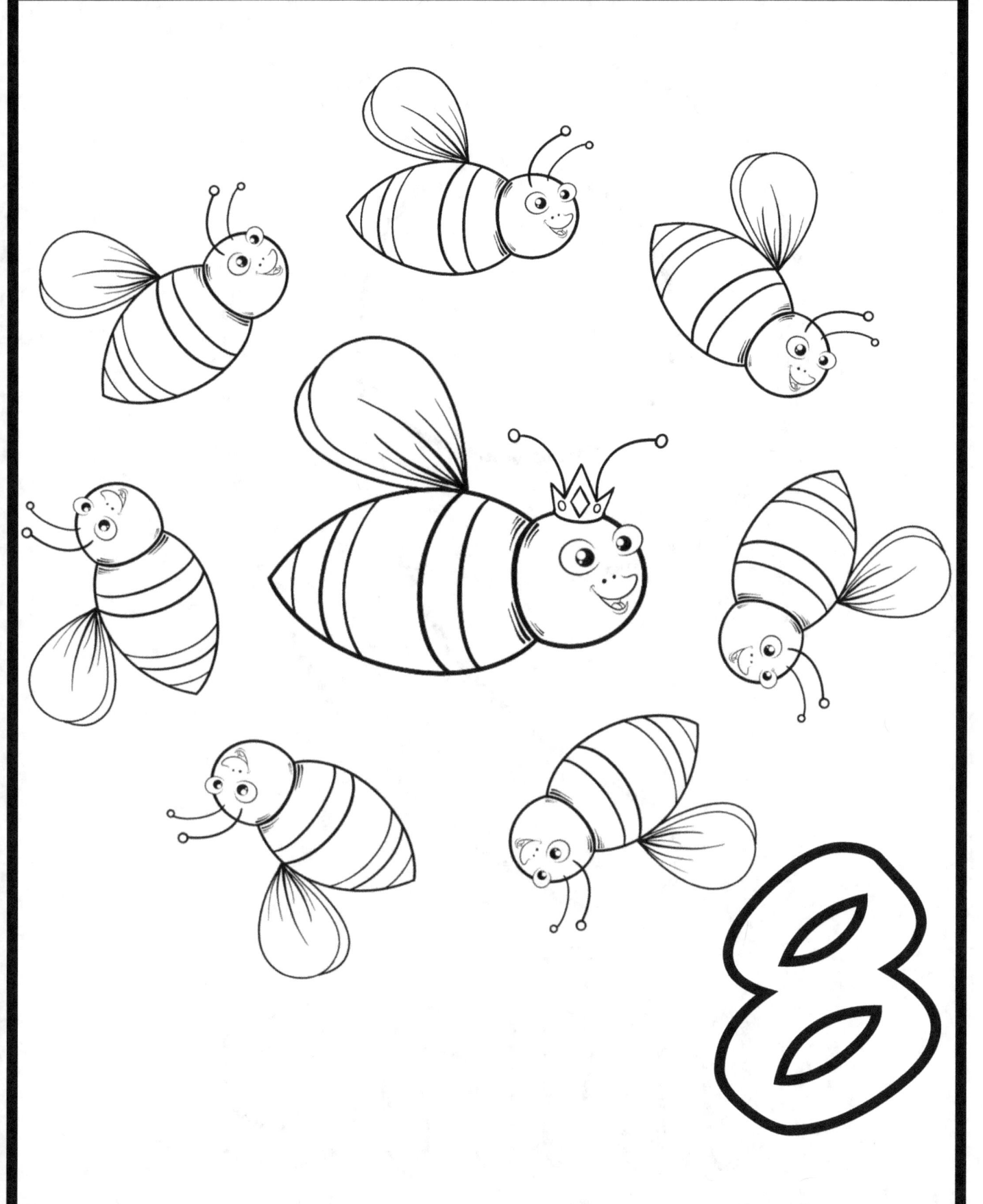

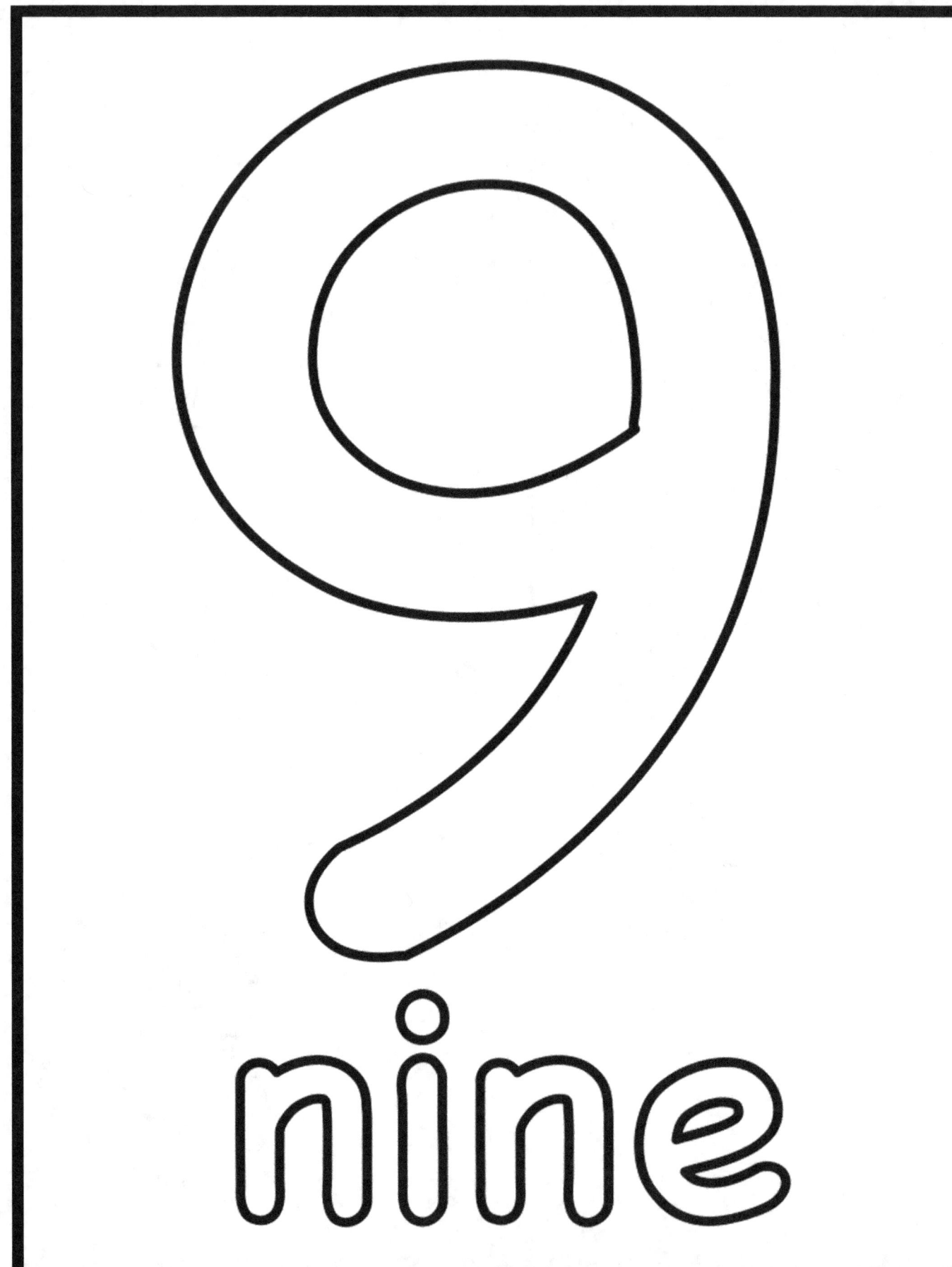

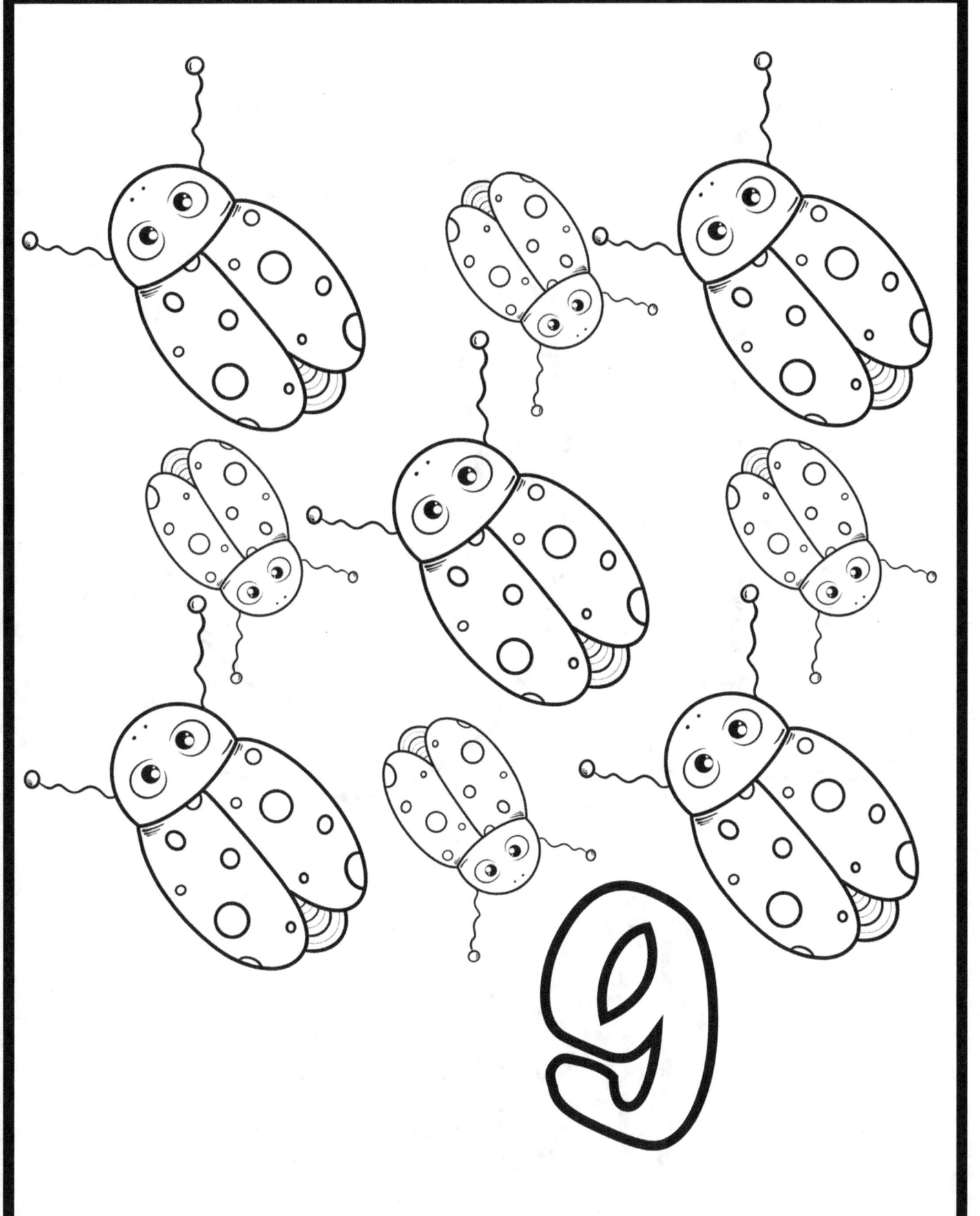

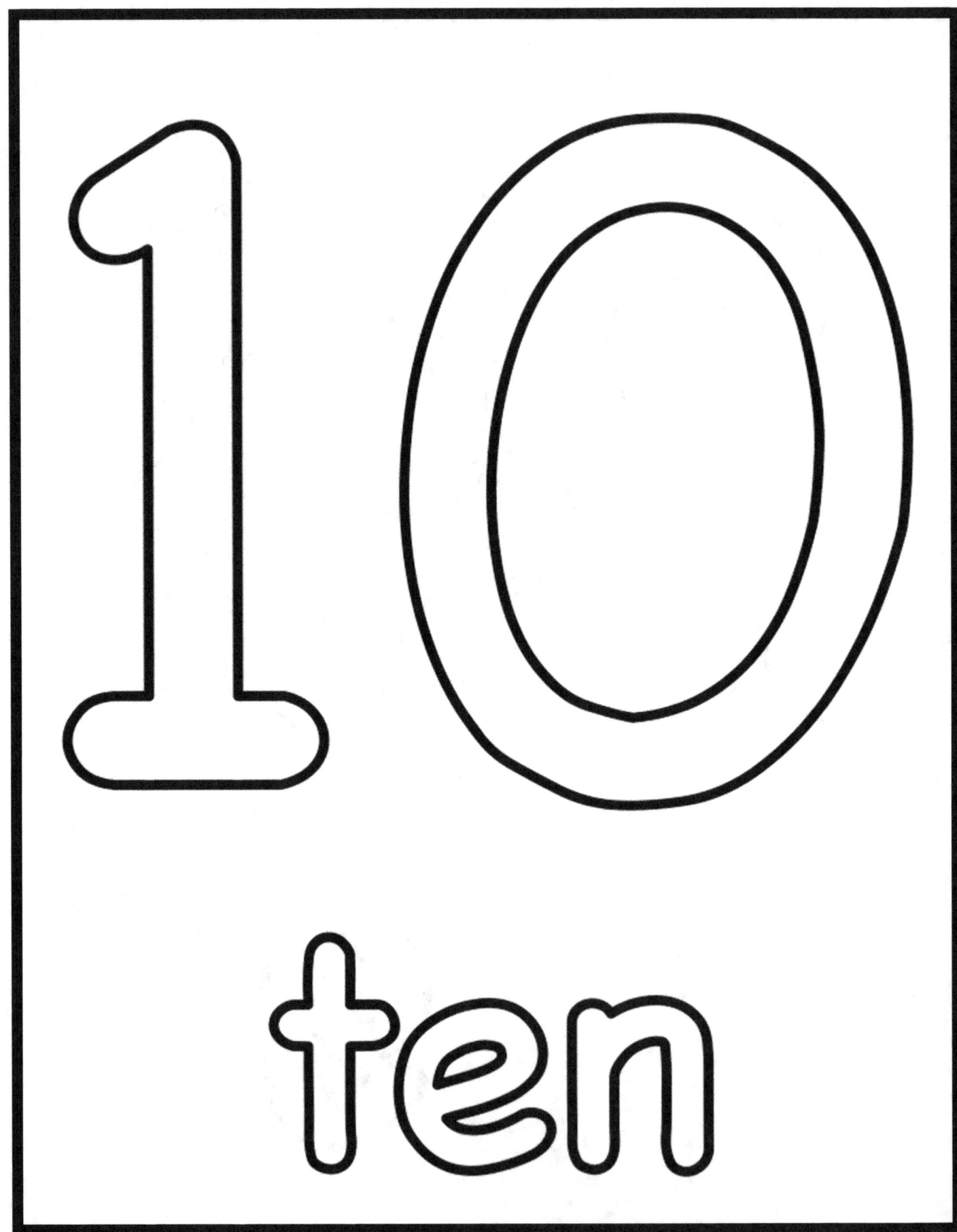

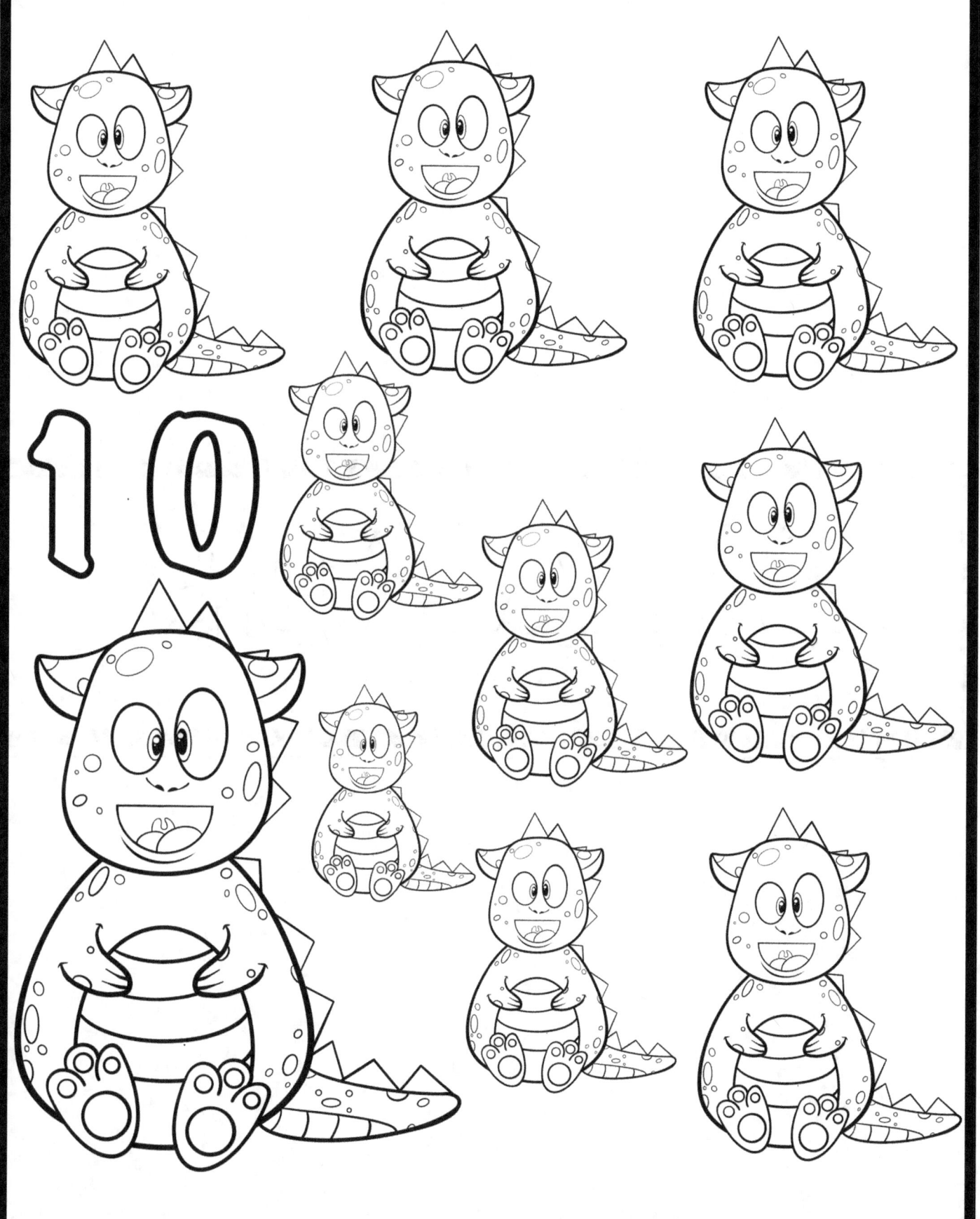

SHAPES

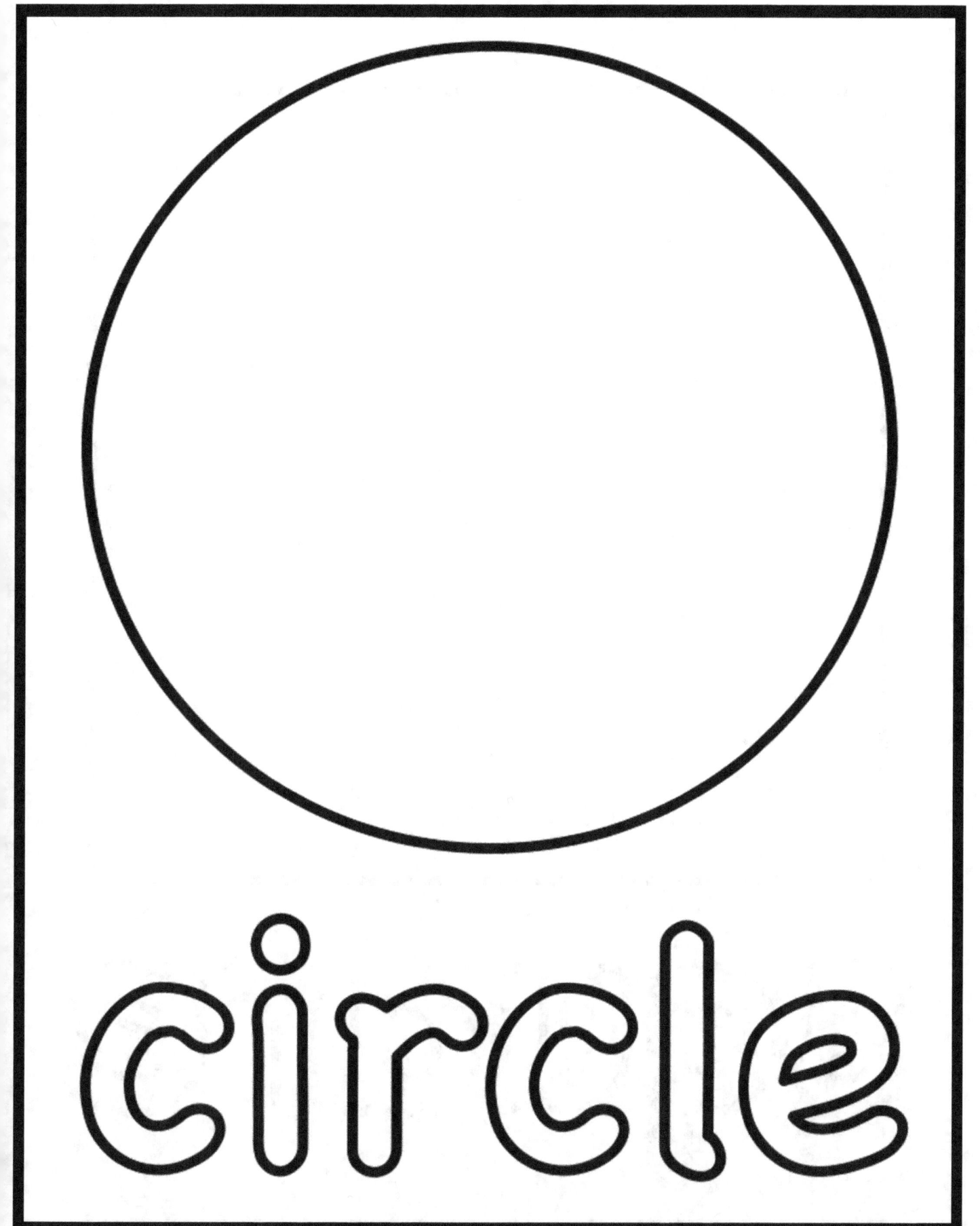

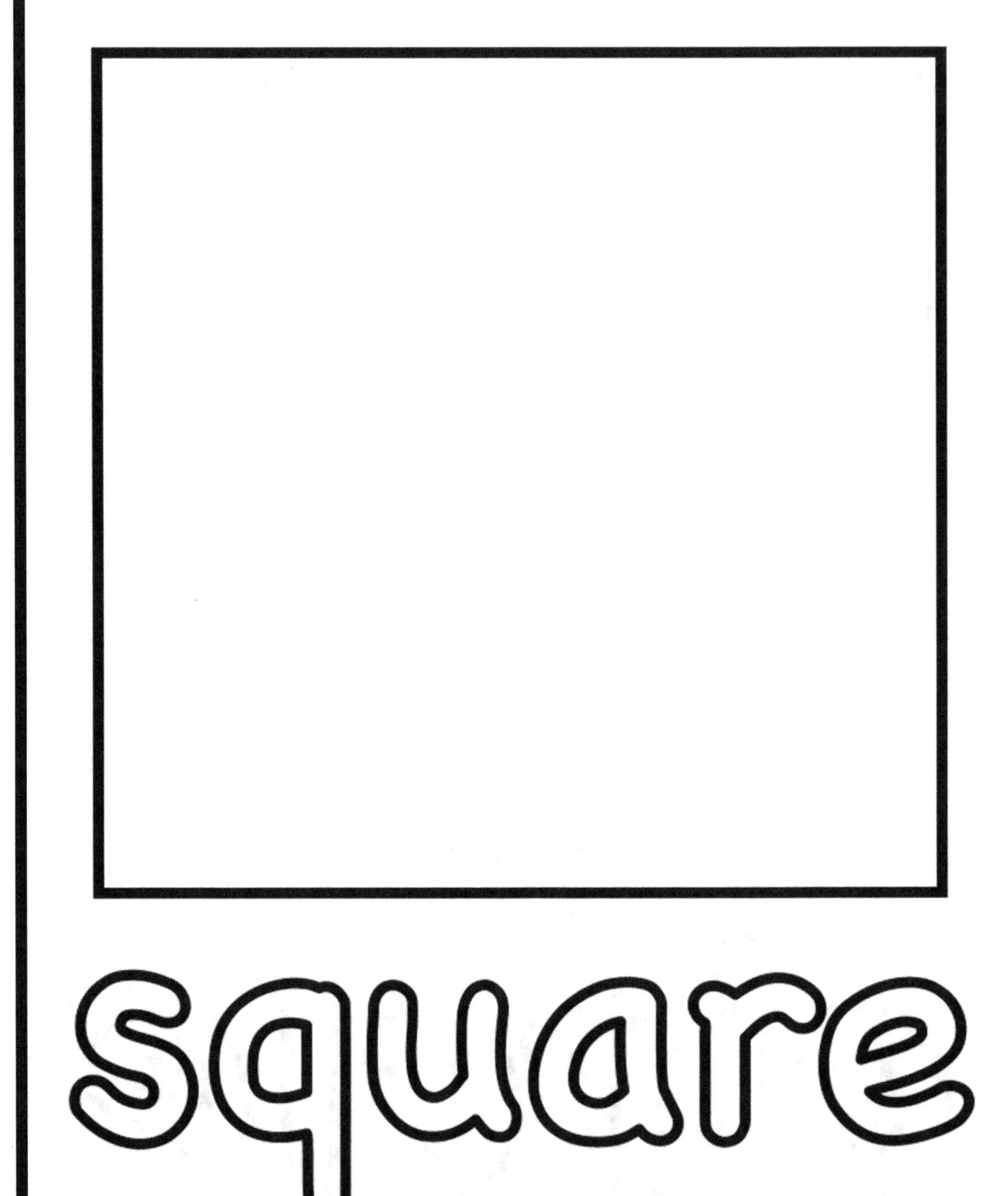

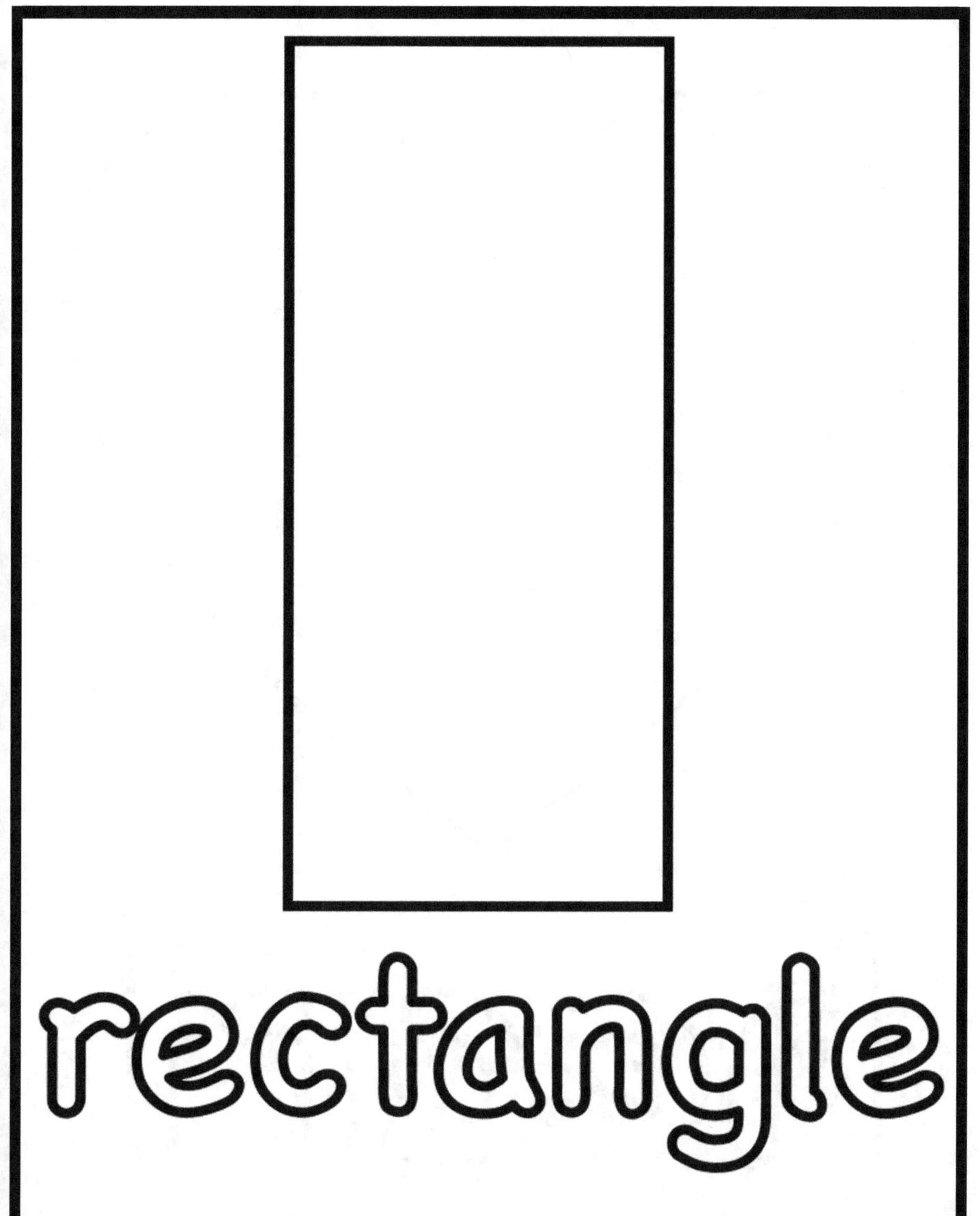

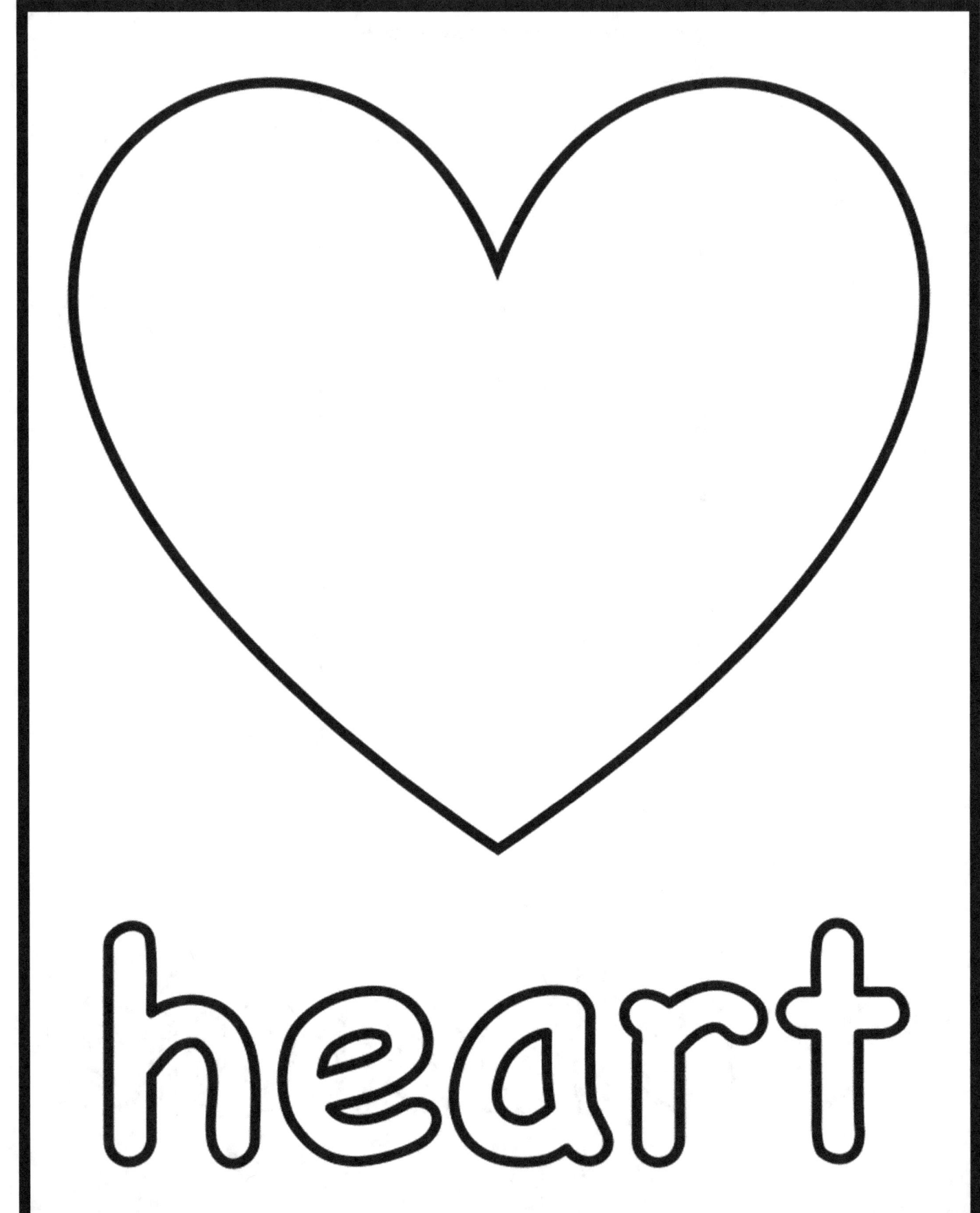

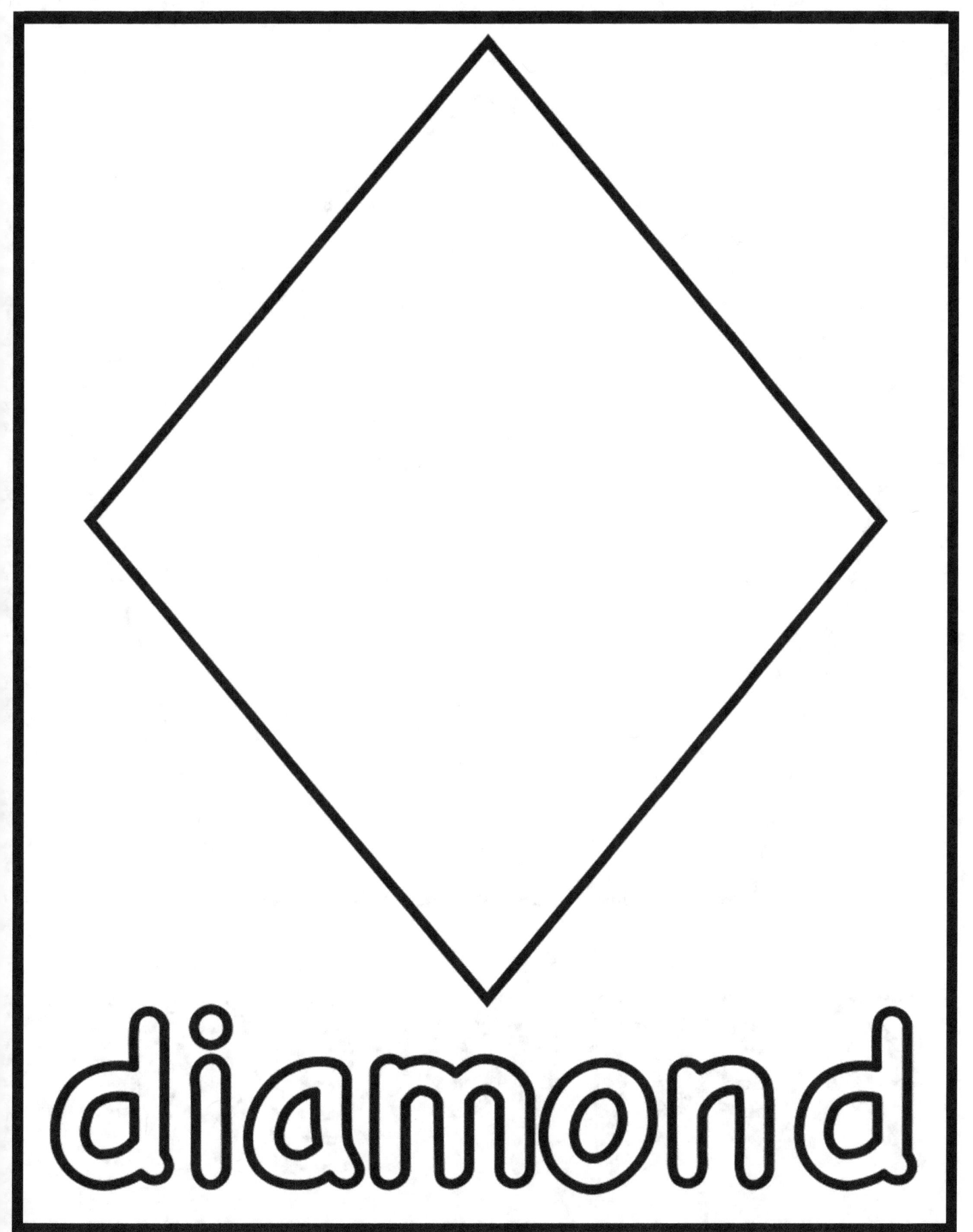

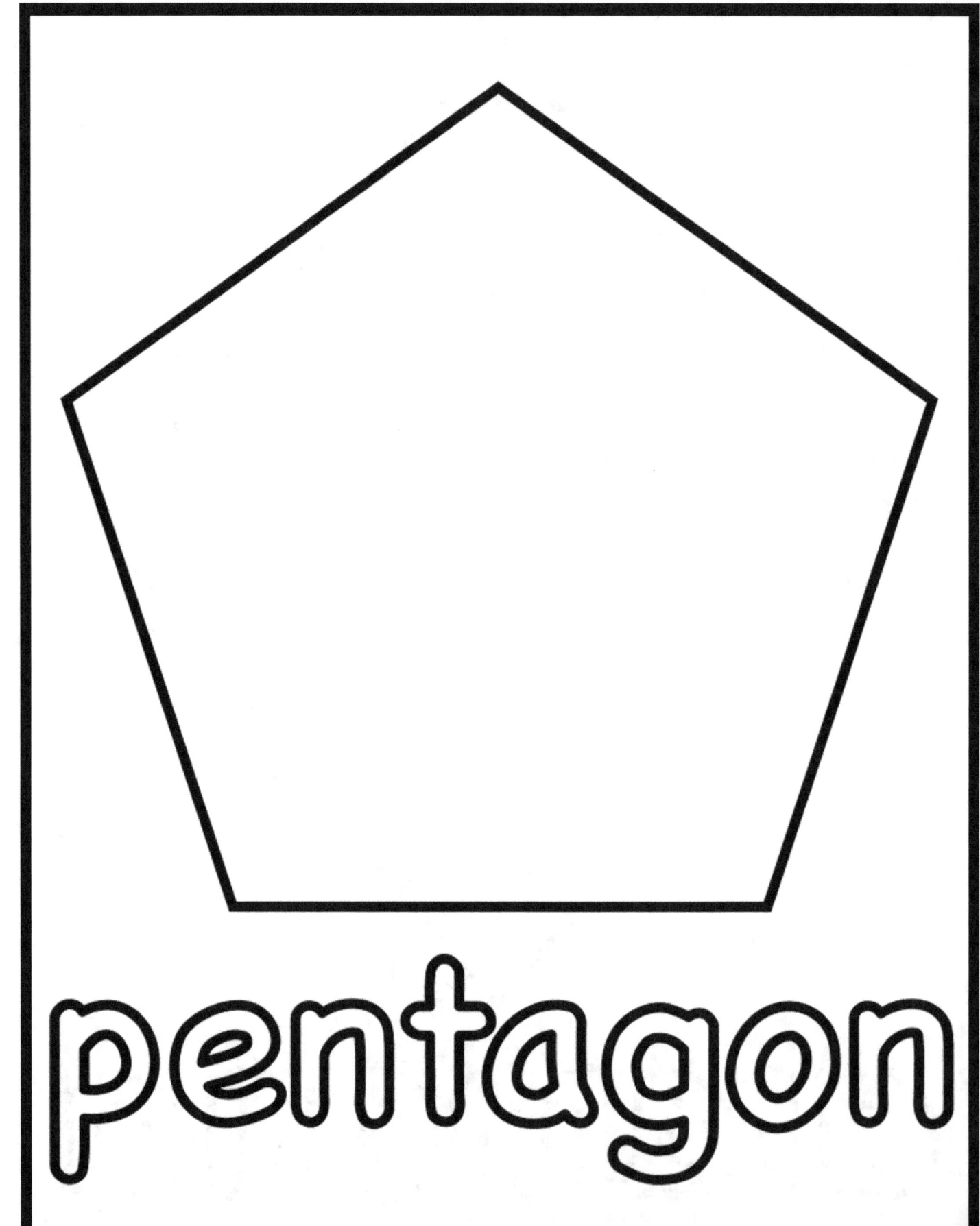

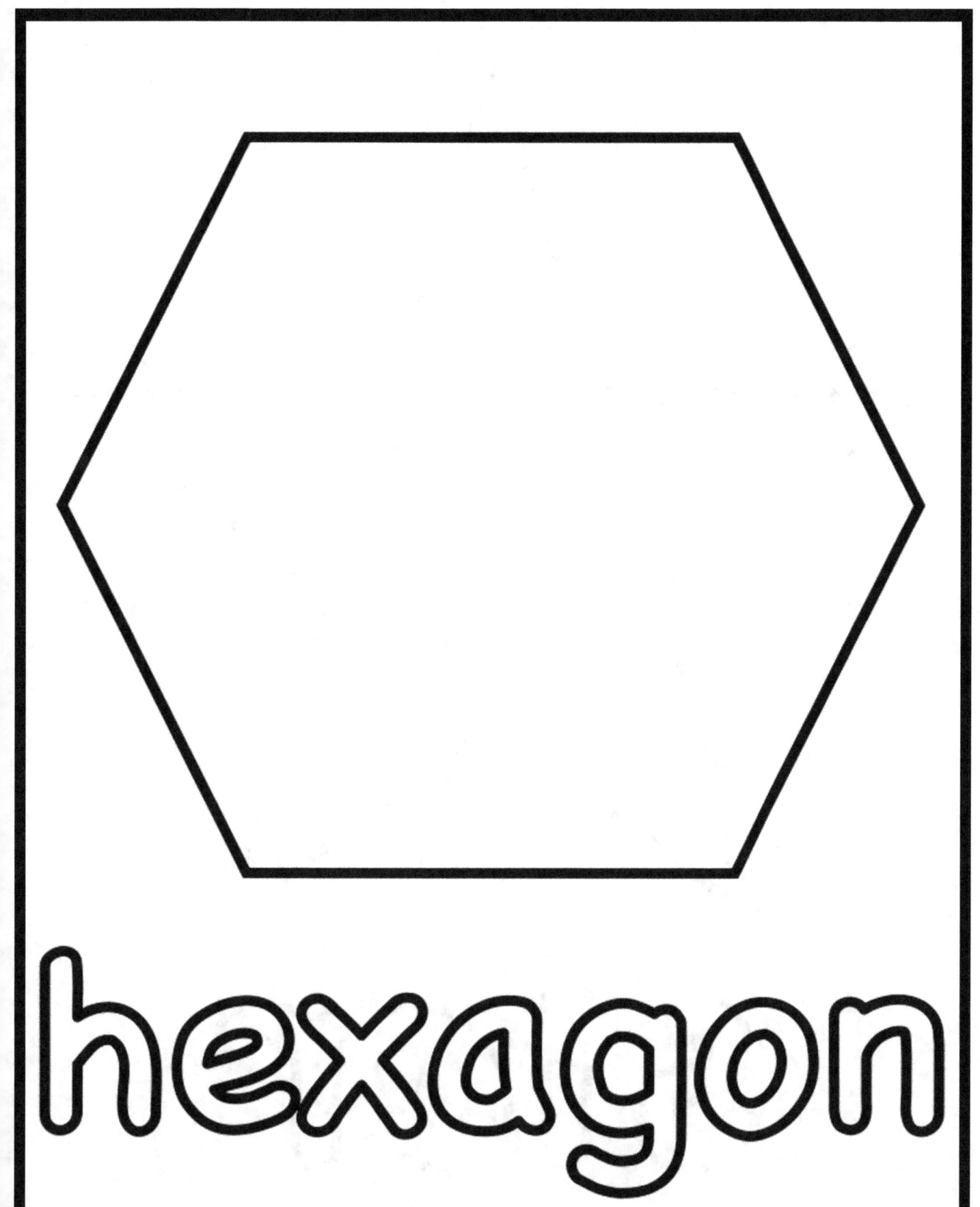

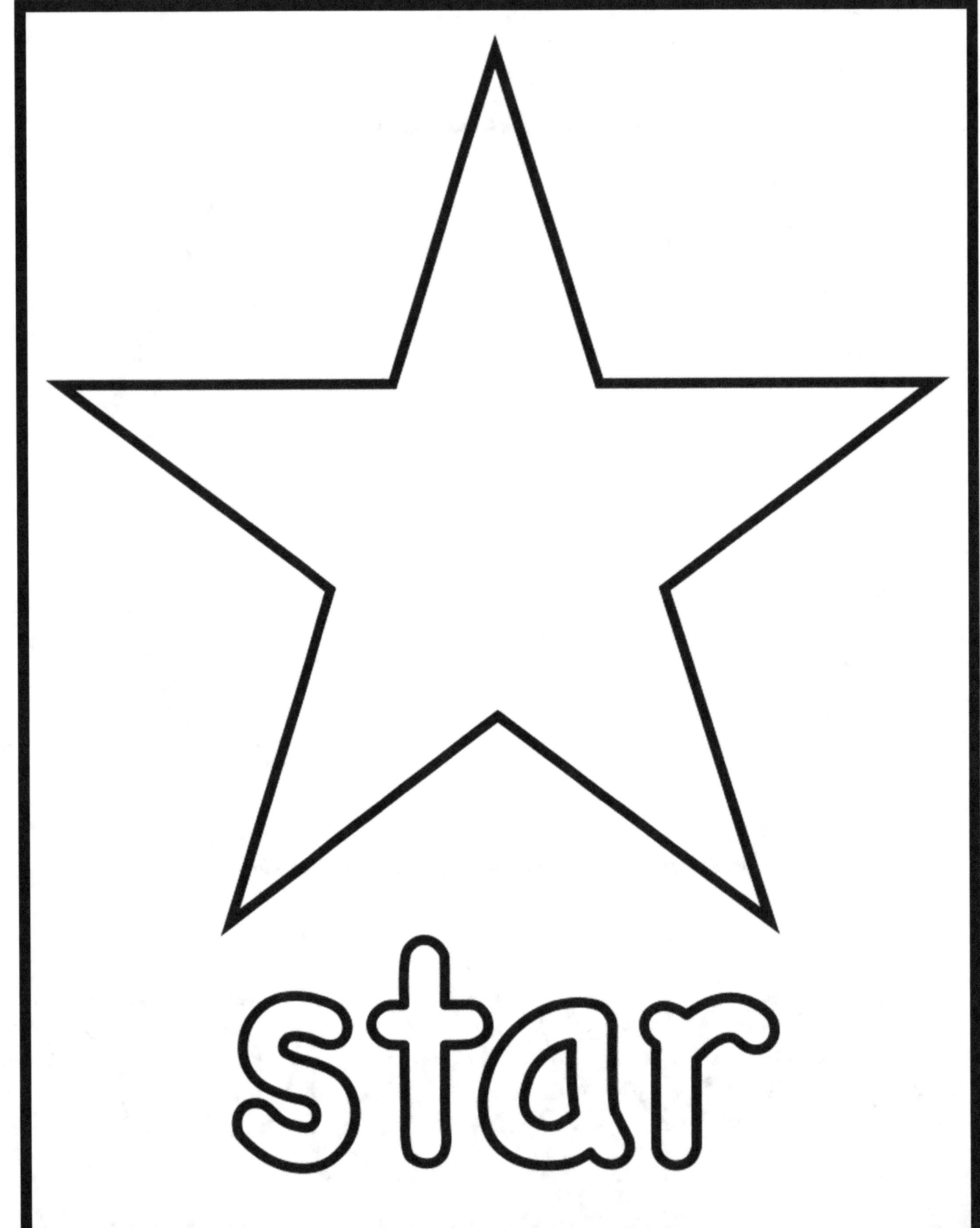

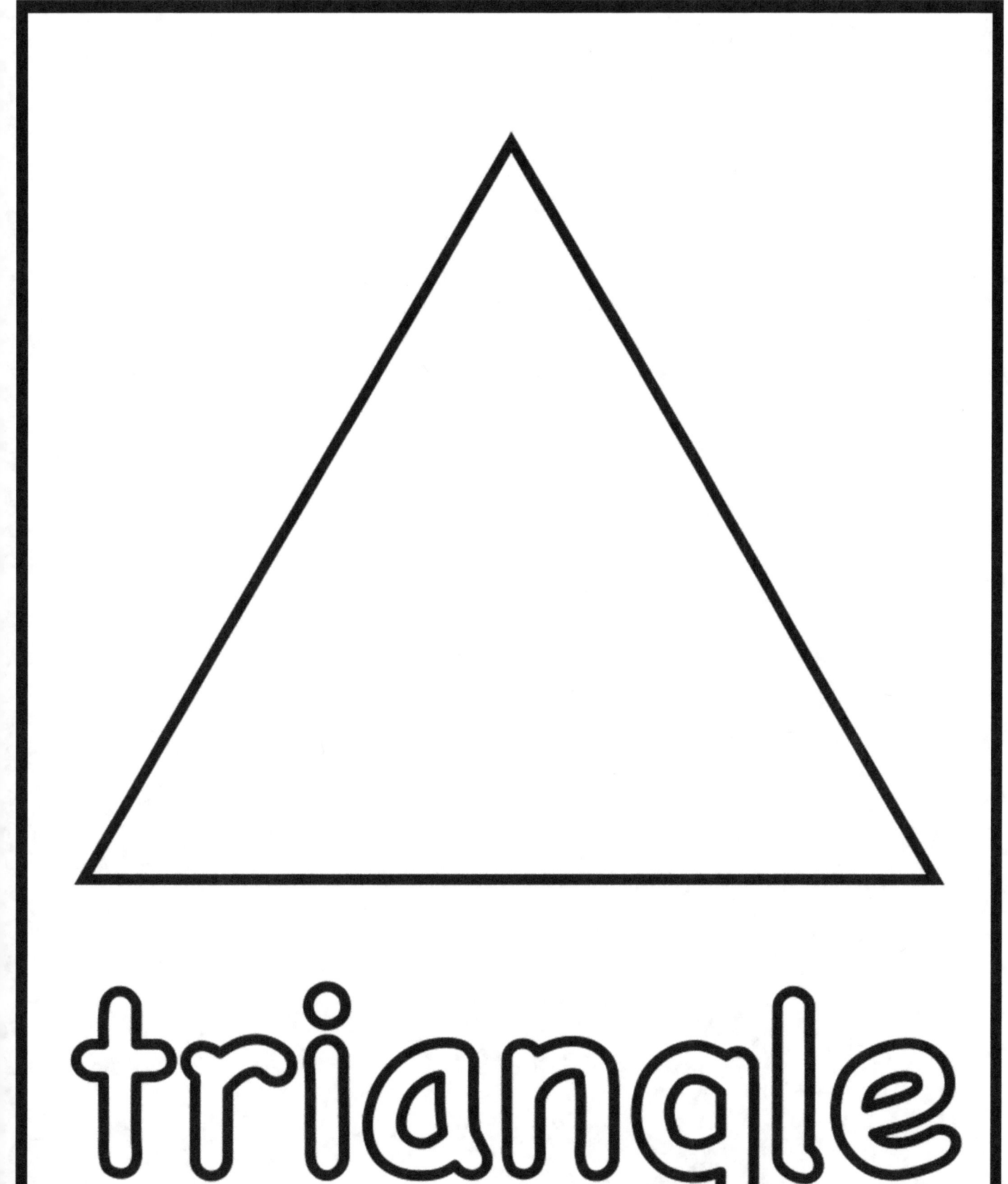

www.ingramcontent.com/pod-product-compliance
Lightning Source LLC
Chambersburg PA
CBHW081436220526
45466CB00008B/2403